IN THE BREEZE
WITH
BIKER GEORGE

IN THE BREEZE WITH BIKER GEORGE

SHORT DAILY RIDE DEVOTIONALS

(Volume 2)

DANO JANOWSKI

Also by Dano Janowski

In The Wind With Biker George: Short Daily Ride Devotionals (Volume 1)

COPYRIGHT PAGE

ACKNOWLEDGMENTS

I wish I could personally thank everyone for their contributions, inspiration, knowledge, & other help in creating volume 2 of the Biker George Daily Ride Devotionals Series. I would never be able to list everyone that has been with me over the course of the years & I would hate to forget to mention someone. Therefore, I would like to publicly acknowledge my two foremost inspirations, my Lord Jesus Christ & my beautiful wife, T.

WHAT PEOPLE ARE SAYING

Biker George is the Voice of Reason that you want in a friend. He speaks truth in a world that doesn't. Having Biker George talking to you daily will keep you out of the ditch and on the road, especially at 200 miles an hour!
Rich Vreeland - Professional Nitro Drag Bike Racer

"Faith comes by hearing, and hearing by the Word of God" and "How shall they hear without a preacher?" Enter Biker George! What a unique, simple, and relative way to reach people from all walks of life with the Word of God. Biker George faces the same challenges and questions we all face in our lives and serves as a way to encourage, strengthen, and correct us thru the application of the Word. By the inspiration of the Holy Spirit, Dano is fulfilling the great commission with this devotional. Great work my brother, I'm sure our Father is well pleased.
Marty Dunkerly - Senior Pastor of Set Free Church Dawsonville, GA & International President of Heaven's Saints Motorcycle Ministry

When I met Dano many years ago I sensed his love, passion and a heart for souls. His enthusiasm for the Lord is truly inspiring. His Biker George Devotionals are for everyone from the white house to the crack house. They are also for those warriors of Christ riding through their journeys on the highways and by-ways of this passing life. These short devotionals will offer you an amazing ride through God's Word.
Rey Perez - The Road Warrior & The Jesus Mailman

Contents

Foreword

Brother Dano has done it again! He's found the perfect blend of what it is to be a biker and what it is to be a believer! With Biker George, Dano takes his readers for a daily ride down the Holy Highway (Isa 35:8). His unforgettable daily devotionals are perfect for all believers on scoots and even for "wannabe believers" too! Biker George's thoughts are deep, but they're always easy to read too. Each devotional is a short message that gets right to the heart of the matter quickly. And as an old friend used to say to me, "That'll preach!" Get ready to ride the Holy Highway with Biker George, Brother Dano and the rest of the crew! Blessings!"

Bro Franko, Founding Pastor of Biker Bible Institute, Christian Biker TV, and Biker Church USA

"Franko"

JANUARY

January 1

Biker George has found that at times he can fool some people about how he really feels. Sometimes a smile & a song may hide the worry, but only God can really lift the anxiety & worry from our hearts.

1 Peter 5:7 (NLT) Give all your worries & cares to God, for he cares about you.

January 2

Biker George once said, If you think nobody cares if you're alive, try missing a couple of bill payments.

Luke 12:7 (NLT) and the very hairs on your head are all numbered. So don't be afraid; you are more valuable to God than a whole flock of sparrows.

January 3

Some people do have a hard time sharing the Gospel with others. However, some of those same people have an easy time sharing gossip with others.

Ephesians 4:29 (GW) Don't say anything that would hurt another person. Instead, speak only what is good so that you can give help wherever it is needed. That way, what you say will help those who hear you.

January 4

Ya know, it's not enough to say a prayer...we have to live it too! Biker George & Angel overheard a conversation between a kid & his dad at the greasy spoon the other day. The dad thanked God for the food in a loud religious self-righteous manner. But when he started eating, he grumbled about the quality of the food & how it was cooked. His kid stopped him & asked "Do you think God heard your prayer & thanks for the food?" "Of course," he replied. "Did He also hear when you grumbled about it just now?"

Matthew 6:5 (MSG) & when you come before God, don't turn that into a theatrical production either. All these people making a regular show out of their prayers, hoping for stardom! Do you think God sits in a box seat?

James 3:9-10 (GW) With our tongues we praise our Lord & Father. Yet, with the same tongues we curse people, who were created in God's likeness. Praise & curses come from the same mouth. My brothers & sisters, this should not happen!

January 5

You ever notice how you can usually tell what club some bikers belong to? Sort of like some kids resemble their parents. We should be resembling our Father God.

1 John 3:1 (KJV) Behold, what manner of love the Father hath bestowed upon us, that we should be called the sons of God...

January 6

Words can build up or words can tear down. Biker George knows we get more done for the Lord when we are working together instead of working against each other.

Psalm 133:1 (KJV) Behold, how good & how pleasant it is for brethren to dwell together in unity!

January 7

Biker George knows God & knows peace. But ya know, with no God there is no peace.

1 Kings 5:4 (MSG) But now God has provided peace all around - no one against us, nothing at odds with us.

January 8

Biker George says that some people are like tea bags. When you see them in hot water you can tell how strong they really are.

Joshua 1:9 (NLT) This is my command - be strong & courageous! Do not be afraid or discouraged. For the Lord your God is with you wherever you go.

January 9

There are people out there who claim to be Christians because they go to church. Regardless of what you say you are, are you living it? Your life, actions, habits, thoughts, talk & more will show who you really are. Biker George says, hang tight with Jesus & He'll hang tight with you & you will become more like Him.

John 13:35 (KJV) By this shall all men know that ye are my disciples, if ye have love one to another.

January 10

Many employers offer health insurance & benefits to full-time, but not part-time workers. Biker George says that this can relate to the spirit realm. Who's your employer? Do you serve sin or God? Are you a full-time Christian or part-time?

Romans 6:13 (NLT) Do not let any part of your body become an instrument of evil to serve sin. Instead, give yourselves completely to God, for you were dead, but now you have new life. So use your whole body as an instrument to do what is right for the glory of God.

January 11

Biker George has learned that the true art of conversation is not just saying the right thing at the right time, but also not saying the wrong thing at the wrong time.

Proverbs 12:18 (GW) Careless words stab like a sword, but the words of wise people bring healing.

January 12

Biker George was out riding when a car veered into his lane & forced him off the road. The car kept going, but George was really shaken. He could have been killed. It ain't sin to feel panic or terror in a life-threatening situation but there is a time for your faith to rise up & to give praises for the Lord's protection. Biker George knows faith & fear. Your faith can run over fear, or your fear can run over faith.

Psalm 56:3 (NLT) But when I am afraid, I will put my trust in you.

January 13

Biker George noticed that after the holidays many go on diets & back to the gym as part of their New Year's resolution. This year instead of focusing on food, let's focus on Bread of Life. While the workouts in the gym will help some, the energy seeking the Lord is a workout that will have lasting benefits now & eternally!

Matthew 4:4 (KJV) It is written, Man shall not live by bread alone, but by every word that proceedeth out of the mouth of God.

1 Timothy 4:8 (KJV) For bodily exercise profiteth little: but godliness is profitable unto all things, having promise of the life that now is, & of that which is to come.

January 14

Biker George went into the club house & asked "Where are y'all gonna spend eternity? Smoking or non-smoking?"

Hebrews 9:27 (KJV) & as it is appointed unto men once to die, but after this the judgment.

January 15

Biker George says, always plan ahead... It wasn't raining when Noah built the ark!

Proverbs 22:3 (NLT) A prudent person foresees danger and takes precautions. The simpleton goes blindly on and suffers the consequences.

January 16

Biker George says that saying the Bible is just a book is like saying "twinkle twinkle little stars" sums up the cosmos.

Psalm 33:6 (GW) The heavens were made by the word of the LORD & all the stars by the breath of his mouth.

January 17

Biker George heard of this young biker on his old sputtering & smoking motorcycle that pulled up to a toll booth. When the Toll collector said "Two dollars". The young biker shouted "Sold!"

Matthew 10:29-31 (MSG) "What's the price of a pet canary? Some loose change, right? & God cares what happens to it even more than you do. He pays even greater attention to you, down to the last detail - even numbering the hairs on your head! So don't be intimidated by all this bully talk. You're worth more than a million canaries.

January 18

Today's mission is to brighten somebody's day with some encouraging words! Don't just read this... Do it! You could be the person who makes an eternal difference in someone's life. We may never know what others are going through or the difference we may make, but God does.

1 Thessalonians 5:11 (KJV) Wherefore comfort yourselves together, & edify one another, even as also ye do.

January 19

Once upon a time there was a small boy attempting to ring the doorbell of a house. However, the boy was short & the doorbell was higher than normal so the little boy could not quite reach it. Biker George noticed him & felt sorry for the kid. So, he stepped up to the porch beside the boy & helped him out by ringing the doorbell repeatedly for the boy. "And now what, young man?" he asked the boy. "Now," the boy said. "We run like crazy!"

Proverbs 25:8 (MSG) Don't jump to conclusions - there may be a perfectly good explanation for what you just saw.

January 20

Let's say you were caught speeding down the highway doing 100 mph. You go to court & just as the judge is about to take your bike away & throw the book at you, someone steps forward & says, "I will pay the fine. I will take the punishment." & you get off, without paying the fine, without any punishment at all. You have been justified, Made right in the eyes of the law. It doesn't change the fact that you were speeding, but the court sees you as innocent. Biker George says, that is what Christ did for us.

Galatians 3:13 (NLT) But Christ has rescued us from the curse pronounced by the law. When he was hung on the cross, he took upon himself the curse for our wrongdoing.

January 21

Cherrapunji, India, is known as the wettest place on earth. The people there actually grow some of their bridges from the roots of rubber trees to get across some of the waters. These living bridges can take around 10 to 15 years to mature & are very stable & can last for hundreds of years. Biker George asks where are our roots? Are we rooted in Jesus? Are we a bridge that leads others to Him?

Colossians 2:7 (NLT) Let your roots grow down into him, & let your lives be built on him. Then your faith will grow strong in the truth you were taught, & you will overflow with thankfulness.

January 22

Biker George & his ole lady had a little disagreement as he was getting ready to ride out on a long road trip. Before he saddles up, he gives her a dozen roses. Eleven are real & one is artificial. He tells his woman "don't cry, I will love you until the last one dies."

Colossians 3:12-14 (GW) As holy people whom God has chosen & loved, be sympathetic, kind, humble, gentle, & patient. Put up with each other, & forgive each other if anyone has a complaint. Forgive as the Lord forgave you. Above all, be loving. This ties everything together perfectly.

January 23

A guy has been riding an old Honda Rebel for several years & finally gets himself a new Harley Ultra Classic Electra Glide. Do you think his neighbors & others who know him will notice the difference? Biker George says, if you weren't saved & then you sincerely gave your life to the Lord & are seeking to be more like Him, people should see the difference!

John 9:8 (NLT) His neighbors & others who knew him as a blind beggar asked each other, "Isn't this the man who used to sit & beg?"

2 Corinthians 5:17 (NLT) This means that anyone who belongs to Christ has become a new person. The old life is gone; a new life has begun!

January 24

A blind beggar is doing his daily asking for food at the gate of temple. Peter & John got something for him that is way more powerful than food or money which is the name of JESUS CHRIST! This forever changed him! Not only was he healed physically, but there was an outward expression, too! Biker George says when you've been with Jesus, others will see Jesus in you!

Acts 3:6-8 (KJV) Peter said, Silver & gold have I none; but such as I have give I thee: In the name of Jesus Christ of Nazareth rise up & walk. And he took him by the right hand, & lifted him up: & immediately his feet & ankle bones received strength. And he leaping up stood, & walked, & entered with them into the temple, walking, & leaping, & praising God!

January 25

On this great adventure called life we ride through the valleys, up the mountains, & around the curves never knowing what's up ahead. The weather & elements can create challenges. Time constraints & real-life situations can put pressure on you. No matter what life deals you, Biker George says, remember to keep the faith & all will work out!

James 1:2-4 (MSG) Consider it a sheer gift, friends, when tests & challenges come at you from all sides. You know that under pressure, your faith-life is forced into the open & shows its true colors. So don't try to get out of anything prematurely. Let it do its work so you become mature & well-developed, not deficient in any way.

January 26

Biker George did have parents that raised him with Christian values. He strayed off the righteous path, but did eventually come back because of their prayers. Keep your kids in prayer to keep the faith or to return to the faith. It's hell out there.

Proverbs 22:6 (KJV) Train up a child in the way he should go: & when he is old, he will not depart from it.

January 27

Have you ever been given an enormous task to accomplish, but not sure if you can accomplish it? Many times in life we are given jobs that seem so big that they appear to be impossible. Biker George says it may appear sometimes that God has given us an overwhelming task, The Great Commission. In other words, we have the task of telling every person on this planet the good news of God's love. We do have support in this effort! HE IS WITH US ALWAYS, even to the end of the age!

Matthew 28:19-20 (NLT) Therefore, go & make disciples of all the nations, baptizing them in the name of the Father & the Son & the Holy Spirit. Teach these new disciples to obey all the commands I have given you. And be sure of this: I am with you always, even to the end of the age."

January 28

Biker George says, we need to love our enemies, not only because the Bible says so, but it will really drive them crazy.

Matthew 5:43-47 (MSG) "You're familiar with the old written law, "Love your friend," & its unwritten companion, "Hate your enemy." I'm challenging that. I'm telling you to love your enemies. Let them bring out the best in you, not the worst. When someone gives you a hard time, respond with the energies of prayer, for then you are working out of your true selves, your God-created selves. This is what God does. He gives his best - the sun to warm & the rain to nourish - to everyone, regardless: the good & bad, the nice & nasty. If all you do is love the lovable, do you expect a bonus? Anybody can do that. If you simply say hello to those who greet you, do you expect a medal? Any run-of-the-mill sinner does that.

January 29

The icy cold nasty weather has caused a lot of bad things to happen across the nation. Biker George was just diagnosed with PMS. They say there is a cure on the horizon for this. Several have been cured when the weather is warmer. Biker George will not wait much longer & will venture out to his shed soon for the cure. The only cure for Parked Motorcycle Syndrome (PMS) is to get out there & ride!

Psalm 147:16-18 (MSG) He spreads snow like a white fleece, he scatters frost like ashes, He broadcasts hail like birdseed - who can survive his winter? Then he gives the command & it all melts; he breathes on winter - suddenly it's spring!

Amos 3:5 (NLT) Does a bird ever get caught in a trap that has no bait? Does a trap spring shut when there's nothing to catch?

January 30

Biker George wonders how can you call God your Father on Sunday at church & then act like an orphan for the rest of the week? He will never abandon you, so don't abandon Him.

Hebrews 13:5b (NLT) God has said, "I will never fail you. I will never abandon you."

January 31

Man's way leads to a hopeless end. God's way leads to an endless hope!

Proverbs 14:12-13 (MSG) There's a way of life that looks harmless enough; look again - it leads straight to hell. Sure, those people appear to be having a good time, but all that laughter will end in heartbreak.

FEBRUARY

February 1

There is a great difference between a worried biker & a concerned biker. The worried frets about the problem, & the concerned solves the problem.

Philippians 4:6-7 (MSG) Don't fret or worry. Instead of worrying, pray. Let petitions & praises shape your worries into prayers, letting God know your concerns. Before you know it, a sense of God's wholeness, everything coming together for good, will come & settle you down. It's wonderful what happens when Christ displaces worry at the center of your life.

February 2

Biker George says duct tape can fix about anything, but it can't fix stupid.

Proverbs 27:22 (MSG) Pound on a fool all you like...you can't pound out foolishness.

February 3

Barry Mayson went from being part of the Hell's Angels to a well-known evangelist & founder of the Heaven's Saints Motorcycle Ministry. Saul went from killing Christians to a well-known evangelist & penned much of the New Testament. Biker George says if Barry & Saul of Tarsus can change for the better, then the Lord can use you too! You have to be willing to surrender to God though!

Acts 9:13-15 (GW) Ananias replied, "Lord, I've heard a lot of people tell about the many evil things this man has done to your people in Jerusalem. Saul has come here to Damascus with authority from the chief priests to put anyone who calls on your name in prison." The Lord told Ananias, "Go! I've chosen this man to bring my name to nations, to kings, & to the people of Israel.

February 4

A man was robbing a Christian Biker's house in the middle of the night & he heard a voice say "Jesus is gonna get you." The robber ignores it, & takes the TV then he hears it again "Jesus is gonna get you." The robber starts to get a little worried & then notices it's just a parrot & says "What's your name, birdie?" "Moses." "What idiot would name you Moses?" "The same idiot who calls his Rottweiler Jesus."

1 Thessalonians 5:2 (NLT) For you know quite well that the day of the Lord's return will come unexpectedly, like a thief in the night.

February 5

Bikers tend to take care of fellow riders. If one is broke down, chances are that they are helped by a brother or we make sure they are OK. It would be great if everyone could take this tradition of biker helping biker & apply it towards everyday life & doing good for others, too.

Galatians 6:9-10 (NLT) So let's not get tired of doing what is good. At just the right time we will reap a harvest of blessing if we don't give up. Therefore, whenever we have the opportunity, we should do good to everyone - especially to those in the family of faith.

February 6

Spending a lot of time with a person or a group of people usually means that you get to know them & they get to know you. You even become more like them whether it be subtle or obvious. Who are you spending time with? Biker George says the more time we spend with Jesus the more we will be Christ like. If we don't invest our time with the Lord, God will still love us no matter what. God loves us but hates sin. Just because He loves everyone doesn't mean everyone is going to heaven. There is hell to pay for sin. Jesus paid the price. For God so loved the world, that He gave His only Son, that whoever believes in Him should not perish but have eternal life.

Romans 8:35 (MSG) Do you think anyone is going to be able to drive a wedge between us & Christ's love for us? There is no way! Not trouble, not hard times, not hatred, not hunger, not homelessness, not bullying threats, not backstabbing, not even the worst sins listed in Scripture

February 7

Biker George says if you wanna be wise ya gotta seek wisdom. Nobody wants to be unwise, but if you're not seeking wisdom, foolishness will find you.

Proverbs 4:7 (KJV) Wisdom is the principal thing; therefore get wisdom: & with all thy getting get understanding.

February 8

A friend gets a great deal on a beautiful used Harley, like new, low miles, with all the bells & whistles. Some of us might start to drool over the once-in-a-lifetime find, be jealous, & wondering why we can't find deals like that. In a nutshell, your bike works fine & it is what you need, & on the other hand, your friend's old bike bit the dust, so he really needed another bike! The Lord supplied his need!

Philippians 4:19 (KJV) But my God shall supply all your need according to his riches in glory by Christ Jesus.

February 9

What is filling your life? Is your life full of love & good things? Biker George says if you let God's Word fill your life, it will show!

Colossians 3:16 (NLT) Let the message about Christ, in all its richness, fill your lives. Teach & counsel each other with all the wisdom he gives. Sing psalms & hymns & spiritual songs to God with thankful hearts.

February 10

Biker George heard it once said that worry is the darkroom in which negatives can develop.

1 Peter 5:7 (NLT) Give all your worries & cares to God, for he cares about you.

February 11

Just like gun control means hitting the target when you shoot, Biker George says God's Word will hit the target too, as long as you share it!

Isaiah 55:11 (KJV) So shall my word be that goeth forth out of my mouth: it shall not return unto me void, but it shall accomplish that which I please , & it shall prosper in the thing whereto I sent it.

February 12

Biker George's saying "The fact that I am a biker doesn't make me a different kinda Christian. But the fact that I am a Christian does make me a different kinda biker." isn't just a saying, it's a lifestyle!

2 Corinthians 6:17 (KJV) Wherefore come out from among them, & be ye separate, saith the Lord, & touch not the unclean thing; & I will receive you.

February 13

Biker George knows that the love that Christ showed us by laying down his life for us is the most powerful example of agape love. Jesus Christ is riding wheel-to-wheel with you so that nothing can come between his love & you.

Romans 8:39 (NLT) No power in the sky above or in the earth below - indeed, nothing in all creation will ever be able to separate us from the love of God that is revealed in Christ Jesus our Lord.

February 14

Angel recently found an old love letter from Biker George that read: "Angel, I'd climb the highest mountain, sail the raging ocean, cross the hottest desert just to see you! PS: I'll be over Saturday night if it doesn't rain."

1 Corinthians 13:7 (NLT) Love never gives up, never loses faith, is always hopeful, & endures through every circumstance.

February 15

Biker George bought a used lawn mower from a yard sale, but it wouldn't run. So he brings it back & lets the guy know. The guy tells George "It'll run, but you have to curse at it to get it started." George was shocked & replied "But I haven't cussed in over 30 years." As the guy walks away he says "Just keep pulling the starter rope, the words will come back to you."

James 1:26 (NLT) If you claim to be religious but don't control your tongue, you are fooling yourself, & your religion is worthless

February 16

Biker George heard this story about an atheist was rowing on Loch Ness in Scotland one day, when suddenly the Loch Ness monster attacked & grabbed him from his boat.

He panicked & shouted "God help me!" & suddenly, the monster & everything around him just froze. A voice from the heavens boomed "You say you don't believe in me, but now you're asking for my help?" The atheist looked up & said, "Well, ten seconds ago I didn't believe in the Loch Ness Monster either."

Ephesians 4:18 (MSG) They've refused for so long to deal with God that they've lost touch not only with God but with reality itself.

February 17

Biker George says knowing God's Word & not sharing it with others is like going out into a battle without putting up a fight.

1 Timothy 6:12 (NLT) Fight the good fight for the true faith. Hold tightly to the eternal life to which God has called you, which you have declared so well before many witnesses.

February 18

Biker George tries to think ahead & has a plan A & B when riding out, just in case of traffic jams or road construction. When he was getting his plans together today he had this thought about how USB sounds like plan B in case the USA fails.

Isaiah 41:10 (AMP) Do not fear [anything], for I am with you; Do not be afraid, for I am your God. I will strengthen you, be assured I will help you; I will certainly take hold of you with My righteous right hand [a hand of justice, of power, of victory, of salvation].

February 19

When you wish upon a star, it makes no difference who you are, it's just a wish that won't go far. Biker George says, why wish you may & why wish you might, when you can pray to the Father of light?

James 1:17 (NLT) Whatever is good & perfect is a gift coming down to us from God our Father, who created all the lights in the heavens. He never changes or casts a shifting shadow.

February 20

Biker George took some pictures of a solar eclipse one time, but they didn't come out good because he wasn't using any filters or special lenses on his camera. Ya know sometimes we might study the word, but the eyes of our understanding can't see a clear picture because we try to do it in the flesh. We need to put on those spiritual lenses & the Holy Spirit will give us the best picture.

2 Corinthians 4:3-4 (MSG) If our Message is obscure to anyone, it's not because we're holding back in any way. No, it's because these other people are looking or going the wrong way & refuse to give it serious attention. All they have eyes for is the fashionable god of darkness. They think he can give them what they want, & that they won't have to bother believing a Truth they can't see. They're stone-blind to the dayspring brightness of the Message that shines with Christ, who gives us the best picture of God we'll ever get.

February 21

Biker George goes to the doctor for a back ache & the doc asks if he's had any recent accidents. George replies "Nope, but last week I was attacked by a dog, scratched by a cat, & bit by a snake." "And you don't call those accidents?" asks the doc. "No, sir," says George... "They all did it on purpose."

Psalm 34:19 (KJV) Many are the afflictions of the righteous: but the Lord delivereth him out of them all.

February 22

Biker George has learned a thing or two in life. One is that he knows there is a God & the other is that he ain't Him.

Hebrews 13:8 (KJV) Jesus Christ the same yesterday, & today, & forever.

February 23

Biker George remembers joyful times when the Lord met his needs in an amazing way. But life has it's hard times too. God's past faithfulness assures us that He'll meet our future needs. That's worth remembering!

Psalm 126:6 (NLT) They weep as they go to plant their seed, but they sing as they return with the harvest.

February 24

The Lord calls us to be salt so that people out there can taste & see that God is good. Biker George says that just like salt makes a difference in the flavor of our food, God's people should make a difference in the world. Ya know the Word of God endures forever, just like salt does. The only thing that will cause salt to lose it's savor is rain or condensation, so don't water down the Gospel when you share it!

Matthew 5:13 (GW) You are salt for the earth. But if salt loses its taste, how will it be made salty again? It is no longer good for anything except to be thrown out & trampled on by people.

February 25

If you have ever gotten really bad lost before & low on fuel, it can be disheartening. Biker George says, imagine your GPS (God's Positioning System) quit & you're riding the wrong way. Then you hear the Lord say "Recalculating... Go to the CROSS, make RIGHT, then go STRAIGHT."

1 Peter 2:24-25 (MSG) He used his servant body to carry our sins to the Cross so we could be rid of sin, free to live the right way. His wounds became your healing. You were lost sheep with no idea who you were or where you were going. Now you're named & kept for good by the Shepherd of your souls.

February 26

Biker George had a Muslim friend that brought him a copy of the Quran on CD. He got really mad when George asked if he could burn a copy.

Galatians 1:8 (NLT) Let God's curse fall on anyone, including us or even an angel from heaven, who preaches a different kind of Good News than the one we preached to you.

February 27

Biker George heard a story about this man robbing a Christian Biker's house in the middle of the night. The thief heard a voice say "Jesus is gonna get you." The robber ignores it, grabs some jewelry & then he hears it again "Jesus is gonna get you." The robber starts to get a little worried & then notices it's just a parrot & says "What's your name, birdie?" "Moses." "What idiot would name you Moses?" "The same idiot who calls his Rottweiler Jesus."

1 Thessalonians 5:2 (NLT) For you know quite well that the day of the Lord's return will come unexpectedly, like a thief in the night.

February 28

Usually when you send an email it gets delivered quickly, but once in a while it takes forever to get to its destination depending on connection or time of day. Sometimes that information superhighway ain't so super. Biker George says that unlike the Internet God is always on time! We can talk to Him any time & He hears more than just our words, He also listens to our hearts.

1 John 5:14 (KJV) & this is the confidence that we have in him, that, if we ask any thing according to his will, he heareth us life.

March 1

Stopping the microwave with just one second left might make you feel like you're the bomb squad & you just saved the world. But in reality, you did save it from beeping. Biker George says, like the microwave, we know our timer on earth is getting ready to beep anytime even though we can't clearly see the numbers.

Romans 13:11 (NLT) This is all the more urgent, for you know how late it is; time is running out. Wake up, for our salvation is nearer now than when we first believed.

March 2

It seems like the older we get, the more we think about the hereafter. Biker George has gone into a room thinking, what did I come in here after?

Colossians 3:2 (NLT) Think about the things of heaven, not the things of earth.

March 3

What if you were in a million-dollar marathon & you had insider info for a guaranteed win? You wouldn't put ankle weights on & ignore the info, but you would follow the instructions for the victory, right? So why do we take on weight of sin & ignore what the Bible says? Biker George says God will show you how to win this spiritual marathon that has an eternal prize that's worth more than millions. Listen to Him!

Hebrews 12:1 (NLT) Therefore, since we are surrounded by such a huge crowd of witnesses to the life of faith, let us strip off every weight that slows us down, especially the sin that so easily trips us up. And let us run with endurance the race God has set before us.

March 4

You never know when you may find the one that needs to hear the Word of God that you share today. Biker George says, keep on keeping on.

Luke 15:7 (KJV) I say unto you, that likewise joy shall be in heaven over one sinner that repenteth, more than over ninety & nine just persons, which need no repentance.

March 5

You can believe in God now or later. Biker George says that here & now is better than the hereafter.

Hebrews 9:27-28 (MSG) Everyone has to die once, then face the consequences. Christ's death was also a one-time event, but it was a sacrifice that took care of sins forever. And so, when he next appears, the outcome for those eager to greet him is, precisely, salvation.

March 6

The first thing we should do when people need help is to pray for them. Biker George says we should never think prayers ain't nothing because our intercession can lead to God's intervention.

James 5:16b (KJV) The effectual fervent prayer of a righteous man availeth much.

March 7

The second you asked to be forgiven, God forgives you. Biker George says, it's then time to ride away from the guilt & quit spinning your tire.

1 John 1:9 (GW) God is faithful & reliable. If we confess our sins, he forgives them & cleanses us from everything we've done wrong.

March 8

Biker George says it's more profitable to watch money change the world than to watch change pile up. If you don't sow seeds, the seeds can't grow.

Luke 19:26 (NLT) ...to those who use well what they are given, even more will be given. But from those who do nothing, even what little they have will be taken away.

March 9

Biker George is getting ready to head out for Daytona. Disney World is about an hour away from there, but then he thought... Disney World is really a people trap run by a mouse.

Amos 3:5 (NLT) Does a bird ever get caught in a trap that has no bait? Does a trap spring shut when there's nothing to catch?

March 10

There is daily bread out there, both physical & spiritual. Biker George says, ain't nobody gonna force feed it to you though. You eat physical food every day. so why not spend some time munching out on a daily devotional that is good for you?

Matthew 6:11 (KJV) Give us this day our daily bread.

March 11

Just because something didn't work out your way it doesn't mean it won't work. Never give up, never surrender says Biker George!

Psalm 31:24 (MSG) Be brave. Be strong. Don't give up. Expect God to get here soon.

March 12

There was a period in time when we use to say "Give me liberty". Biker George has noticed that now days many just say "Give me".

1 Corinthians 10:24 (NLT) Don't be concerned for your own good but for the good of others.

March 13

We all see that there is a lot of bad stuff going on in the world with the shootings, protests, terrorist attacks, etc. This what the news & media is sharing with everyone to see & hear. Biker George says that while we can't ignore it, we don't want to dwell on it. While some are fearful & hide, we need to pray & stay as we are lights in the darkness.

1 Thessalonians 5:16-18 (MSG) Be cheerful no matter what; pray all the time; thank God no matter what happens. This is the way God wants you who belong to Christ Jesus to live.

March 14

If God is really important in our lives, then we should be less important than He is. Biker George says it's all about Him, not all about us.

John 3:30 (GW) He must increase in importance, while I must decrease in importance.

March 15

There is so much bad news that the world is hearing now days. Biker George says it's time to tell the world some good news!

1 Chronicles 16:8 (MSG) Thank God! Call out his Name! Tell the whole world who he is & what he's done!

March 16

Biker George says that you can't get to your destination if you don't get on your bike & ride.

Philippians 1:6 (NLT) & I am certain that God, who began the good work within you, will continue his work until it is finally finished on the day when Christ Jesus returns.

March 17

Biker George says there are two days we shouldn't worry about, yesterday & tomorrow. Ya know, yesterday is history & tomorrow is a mystery.

Matthew 6:34 (MSG) Give your entire attention to what God is doing right now, & don't get worked up about what may or may not happen tomorrow. God will help you deal with whatever hard things come up when the time comes.

March 18

Biker George says that you can't get to your destination if you don't get on your bike & ride.

Philippians 1:6 (NLT) & I am certain that God, who began the good work within you, will continue his work until it is finally finished on the day when Christ Jesus returns.

March 19

Biker George says that while death may seem like it's the last chapter in time, it's only the first page on the road of eternity.

Revelation 21:4 (NLT) He will wipe every tear from their eyes, & there will be no more death or sorrow or crying or pain. All these things are gone forever.

March 20

Biker George says that a challenging road through life can lead to an awesome destination.

James 1:12 (GW) Blessed are those who endure when they are tested. When they pass the test, they will receive the crown of life that God has promised to those who love him.

March 21

Some people think good character means a good Halloween costume character. Biker George knows that being a person of good character means having a heart of integrity.

Matthew 12:33 (NLT) A tree is identified by its fruit. If a tree is good, its fruit will be good. If a tree is bad, its fruit will be bad.

March 22

Biker George, like some others, watch the Weather Channel & watch the sky so they know what the weather is gonna be. Why can't people read the Bible & read the signs of the times so they know that the Lord is coming back soon?

Matthew 16:3 (GW) & in the morning you say that there will be a storm today because the sky is red & overcast. You can forecast the weather by judging the appearance of the sky, but you cannot interpret the signs of the times.

March 23

We all get to ride this road called life, & if you're reading this, you're still alive. Biker George says on this road it's not always all about the person who gets the most years in their life, but the person who gets the most life in their years.

John 10:10 (KJV) The thief cometh not, but for to steal, & to kill, & to destroy: I am come that they might have life, & that they might have it more abundantly.

March 24

Biker George says we need to taste our words before we spit them out. What you say flows from what's in your heart.

Proverbs 4:23-27 (MSG) Keep vigilant watch over your heart; that's where life starts. Don't talk out of both sides of your mouth; avoid careless banter, white lies, & gossip. Keep your eyes straight ahead; ignore all sideshow distractions. Watch your step, & the road will stretch out smooth before you. Look neither right nor left; leave evil in the dust.

March 25

Being an example ain't just something that influences others. Biker George says it's the main thing. Young or old... Be a good example!

1 Timothy 4:12 (NLT) Don't let anyone think less of you because you are young. Be an example to all believers in what you say, in the way you live, in your love, your faith, & your purity.

March 26

Biker George is getting ready to go for a morning ride & almost forgot his helmet. Don't forget that the one helmet that you gotta have to ride with Christ is that helmet of salvation.

Ephesians 6:17 (KJV) & take the helmet of salvation, & the sword of the Spirit, which is the word of God

March 27

Reading & studying the Bible is a good thing. However, Biker George says that Bible study is not just to inform us, it's supposed to transform us.

Romans 12:2 (KJV) & be not conformed to this world: but be ye transformed by the renewing of your mind, that ye may prove what is that good, & acceptable, & perfect, will of God.

March 28

Both Biker George & his ole lady have favorites they watch on TV. However, they really didn't care for each other's shows. George loves Angel more than TV, so part of the way he shows his love is by watching her shows by her side. Now he likes them shows too! Ya know, we need to show love for others as Jesus showed His love for us.

John 13:34 (NLT) So now I am giving you a new commandment: Love each other. Just as I have loved you, you should love each other.

March 29

Biker George was filling up his bike with gas & it overflowed on his tank, motor & all over... not good. Ya know when the Lord fills us with His hope, joy & peace, it should be overflowing onto all those near us... That's good stuff there!

Romans 15:13 (NLT) I pray that God, the source of hope, will fill you completely with joy & peace because you trust in him. Then you will overflow with confident hope through the power of the Holy Spirit.

March 30

Voice activation technology is pretty cool. Many of us can trigger our smartphones & GPS to action just by speaking to them. Biker George knows that in the spiritual realm, we also have voice activated faith!

2 Corinthians 4:13 (NLT) But we continue to preach because we have the same kind of faith the psalmist had when he said, "I believed in God, so I spoke."

March 31

Biker George knows many who are in a custody battle. It's a spiritual custody battle between Satan & the Lord. God doesn't want just weekend visitations... He wants full custody. Good news is that you get to choose who you will stay with.

Deuteronomy 30:19 (NLT) Today I have given you the choice between life & death, between blessings & curses. Now I call on heaven & earth to witness the choice you make. Oh, that you would choose life, so that you & your descendants might live!

April 1
Biker George says the danger of shooting from the hip is getting shot in the foot.
Proverbs 29:11 (NLT) Fools vent their anger, but the wise quietly hold it back.

April 2
Biker George says you don't alter God's Word to fit your lifestyle, you alter your lifestyle to fit God's Word.
Romans 12:2 (KJV) & be not conformed to this world: but be ye transformed by the renewing of your mind, that ye may prove what is that good, & acceptable, & perfect, will of God.

April 3
Biker George says that being still & waiting on God is still doing something.
Psalm 37:7 (AMP) Be still before the Lord; wait patiently for Him & entrust yourself to Him; Do not fret (whine, agonize) because of him who prospers in his way, Because of the man who carries out wicked schemes.

April 4

Nothing in this world likens to the gifts of God's love & forgiveness. If the pleasures of this world are preventing you from trusting in Jesus Christ, please think again. It's not worth the cost of your eternal soul. Biker George knows that Jesus is the only fountain who can satisfy a thirsty soul.

Matthew 16:26 (NLT) & what do you benefit if you gain the whole world but lose your own soul? Is anything worth more than your soul?

April 5

Life, love, & chocolate taste best when we share it with others. Biker George says sharing is caring.

Ephesians 5:1-2 (MSG) Watch what God does, & then you do it, like children who learn proper behavior from their parents. Mostly what God does is love you. Keep company with him & learn a life of love. Observe how Christ loved us. His love was not cautious but extravagant. He didn't love in order to get something from us but to give everything of himself to us. Love like that.

April 6

Biker George was remembering the story of "The Little Engine That Could" & how it climbed the steep hill saying, "I think I can. I think I can" & then "I know I can. I know I can." Ya know, if you have Jesus Christ as your Lord & Savior, you can say, "I know I can. I know I can" because of Jesus.

Philippians 4:13 (NLT) For I can do everything through Christ, who gives me strength.

Ephesians 3:20 (NLT) Now all glory to God, who is able, through his mighty power at work within us, to accomplish infinitely more than we might ask or think.

April 7

Biker George enjoys his ride with the Lord & he cannot be swayed because they are riding wheel to wheel with each other.

Psalm 16:8 (NLT) I know the Lord is always with me. I will not be shaken, for he is right beside me

April 8
Biker George says that sharing the Gospel is sorta like one beggar telling another beggar where to find bread.
Romans 10:13 (KJV) For whosoever shall call upon the name of the Lord shall be saved.

April 9
Biker George says that the most important investments you can make is time spent with the Lord & your kids.
Psalm 127:3 (GW) Children are an inheritance from the Lord. They are a reward from him.

April 10
If you going through a storm in your life or hurricane force winds & rain, Biker George says we can call out to the Lord & he can calm the storm & bring us through it.
Psalms 107:28-29 (GW) In their distress they cried out to the Lord . He led them from their troubles. He made the storm calm down, & the waves became still.

April 11
Are you ready for what God may want you to do? When the Spirit says, "Go," will you be ready? Biker George says we need to keep our tools ready. God will find work for us!
Galatians 6:2 (AMP) Carry one another's burdens & in this way you will fulfill the requirements of the law of Christ [that is, the law of Christian love].

April 12
Biker George knows some who have iPods, iPhones, iThis & iThat. But ya know, George is old school. He says "iRock for King Jesus!"
Psalm 33:3 (KJV) Sing unto him a new song; play skillfully with a loud noise.

April 13
Biker George says don't be a poser! Being a real Christian is like being a real Biker. It's not what you wear or where you attend church, it's in your heart & soul, & it shows by how you live your public & private life. You can fool some of the people some of the time, but you can't fool God.

Isaiah 29:13-14 (MSG) The Master said: "These people make a big show of saying the right thing, but their hearts aren't in it. Because they act like they're worshiping me but don't mean it, I'm going to step in & shock them awake, astonish them, stand them on their ears. The wise ones who had it all figured out will be exposed as fools. The smart people who thought they knew everything will turn out to know nothing."

April 14
Biker George asks that when the Holy Spirit speaks to your heart to repent, will you ride with Jesus in the light or ride solo in the dark?

Acts 3:19 (KJV) Repent ye therefore, & be converted, that your sins may be blotted out, when the times of refreshing shall come from the presence of the Lord.

April 15
Biker George was riding to the CPA to get his taxes done. Ya know, death & taxes are inevitable, but death doesn't repeat itself!

Matthew 22:21 (NLT) ..."give to Caesar what belongs to him. But everything that belongs to God must be given to God."

Hebrews 9:27 (NLT) And just as each person is destined to die once and after that comes judgment.

April 16
Biker George looks as life like it's a ride with God. It may be hard at times but ya know, it will be well worth it!

Psalm 84:5-7 (MSG) & how blessed all those in whom you live, whose lives become roads you travel; They wind through lonesome valleys, come upon brooks, discover cool springs & pools brimming with rain! God-traveled, these roads curve up the mountain, & at the last turn - Zion! God in full view!

April 17

Biker George says that some of the best exercise is to reach out & lift people up.

Hebrews 13:16 (GW) Don't forget to do good things for others & to share what you have with them. These are the kinds of sacrifices that please God.

April 18

Biker George says you can learn a lot from those who walk close to the Lord, then ya got to share it with others.

2 Timothy 2:2 (GW) You've heard my message, & it's been confirmed by many witnesses. Entrust this message to faithful individuals who will be competent to teach others.

April 19

Biker George says he feels like sometimes he's upside down, his nose is running & his feet are smelling.

Psalm 119:143-144 (MSG) Even though troubles came down on me hard, your commands always gave me delight. The way you tell me to live is always right; help me understand it so I can live to the fullest.

April 20

Biker George says the best way to git er done is to work like you're working for the Lord rather than for people.

Colossians 3:23 (KJV) & whatsoever ye do, do it heartily, as to the Lord, & not unto men

April 21

Biker George says you can be a good person. Get practiced up.

Luke 6:45 (KJV) A good man out of the good treasure of his heart bringeth forth that which is good; & an evil man out of the evil treasure of his heart bringeth forth that which is evil: for of the abundance of the heart his mouth speaketh.

April 22

Biker George says it's a good thing when you put others first, after all, Jesus put us first when he gave his life for us.

Philippians 2:3-4 (KJV) Let nothing be done through strife or vainglory; but in lowliness of mind let each esteem other better than themselves. Look not every man on his own things, but every man also on the things of others.

April 23

To succeed we can't just stare up the steps. Biker George says ya need to step up the stairs!

Proverbs 16:3 (NLT) Commit your actions to the Lord, & your plans will succeed.

April 24

Changing oil in the motorcycle & the Lucas High Performance Synthetic 20W50 looked to be the best. However, Biker George says the best oil you can use in life is some elbow grease.

Colossians 3:23 (KJV) & whatsoever ye do, do it heartily, as to the Lord, & not unto men

April 25

Biker George says that before you stand firm, be sure your feet are in the right place.

Ephesians 6:13 (KJV) Wherefore take unto you the whole armour of God, that ye may be able to withstand in the evil day, & having done all, to stand.

April 26

When you are saved, you become a new person. Biker George says that means the old life is gone & you have a new life in Jesus!

2 Corinthians 5:17 (KJV) Therefore if any man be in Christ, he is a new creature: old things are passed away; behold, all things are become new.

April 27

Biker George had a dream & the Lord told him not to be scared or quiet, but to keep on talking to them other bikers & folks!

Acts 18:9 (NLT) One night the Lord spoke to Paul in a vision & told him, "Don't be afraid! Speak out! Don't be silent!

April 28

Biker George isn't always accepted as a minister because he looks like a biker. We shouldn't judge a book by its cover, but ya know sometimes a book's cover can give you a hint of what it's about. In the end it's about the contents & the author of the book. Got Jesus?

2 Corinthians 10:7-8 (MSG) You stare & stare at the obvious, but you can't see the forest for the trees. If you're looking for a clear example of someone on Christ's side, why do you so quickly cut me out? Believe me, I am quite sure of my standing with Christ. You may think I overstate the authority he gave me, but I'm not backing off. Every bit of my commitment is for the purpose of building you up, after all, not tearing you down.

April 29

Biker George has noticed something missing in the lives of several of God's people... JOY. God's desire is that we would experience fullness of JOY with Him as our road captain.

Psalm 16:11 (GW) You make the path of life known to me. Complete joy is in your presence. Pleasures are by your side forever.

April 30

Biker George says that life is too short to be at war with others. We all need to work at getting along with each other & giving peace a chance.

Hebrews 12:14 (GW) Try to live peacefully with everyone, & try to live holy lives, because if you don't, you will not see the Lord.

May 1

Biker George asks "What is in the center of your life? Is it TV, your bike, or stuff?" If it is Christ, then there is hope. Know God know hope, no God no hope.

Revelation 7:17 (KJV) For the Lamb which is in the midst of the throne shall feed them, & shall lead them unto living fountains of waters: & God shall wipe away all tears from their eyes.

May 2

Biker George says whatever you do, wherever you ride, be riding like the Lord is riding side by side with you.

Colossians 3:23 (NLT) Work willingly at whatever you do, as though you were working for the Lord rather than for people.

May 3
God's word is alive & powerful, but it ain't gonna do anything if you just keep it on the shelf. Biker George says we need to study it & share it!

Hebrews 4:12 (GW) God's word is living & active. It is sharper than any two-edged sword & cuts as deep as the place where soul & spirit meet, the place where joints & marrow meet. God's word judges a person's thoughts & intentions.

May 4
Biker George says whatever you ride, ride it with your whole heart for the Lord's work.

Colossians 3:23 (KJV) & whatsoever ye do, do it heartily, as to the Lord, & not unto men;

May 5
Smokey the Bear says only YOU can prevent forest fires. Biker George would like to remind you that it's easier to start a fire than to put it out.

James 3:6 (MSG) It only takes a spark, remember, to set off a forest fire. A careless or wrongly placed word out of your mouth can do that. By our speech we can ruin the world, turn harmony to chaos, throw mud on a reputation, send the whole world up in smoke & go up in smoke with it, smoke right from the pit of hell.

May 6
Biker George loves Rock & Roll. He is standing on the Rock & his name is on the roll!

Psalm 62:6 (AMP) He only is my rock & my salvation; My fortress & my defense, I will not be shaken or discouraged.

May 7
Biker George says we can always ride in confidence with the Lord as our road captain!

Deuteronomy 31:8 (GW) The Lord is the one who is going ahead of you. He will be with you. He won't abandon you or leave you. So don't be afraid or terrified.

May 8

The eagle has no fear of danger. Biker George says we need to be like the eagle, especially with God on our side. We can be fearless!

Psalm 27:1 (MSG) Light, space, zest - that's God! So, with him on my side I'm fearless, afraid of no one & nothing.

May 9

Biker George says when we are weak HE is strong & when we seek & find HIM we are strong! When should we seek the Lord? ALWAYS!!!

1 Chronicles 16:11 (KJV) Seek the Lord & his strength, seek his face continually.

May 10

Biker George says that often times the reward of something well done is to have done it.

Ephesians 6:8 (NLT) Remember that the Lord will reward each one of us for the good we do, whether we are slaves or free.

May 11

Biker George says that some goals start as dreams.

Acts 2:17 (NLT) "In the last days," God says, "I will pour out my Spirit upon all people. Your sons & daughters will prophesy. Your young men will see visions, & your old men will dream dreams."

May 12

Biker George says when riding, don't be in such a hurry to get to the next stop because you could end up in the next world.

Romans 8:25 (NLT) But if we look forward to something we don't yet have, we must wait patiently & confidently.

May 13

Patience is waiting without worrying says Biker George.

Romans 12:12 (KJV) Rejoicing in hope; patient in tribulation; continuing instant in prayer;

May 14
Biker George was gonna retire but that would mean no more days off!

Philippians 1:6 (GW) I'm convinced that God, who began this good work in you, will carry it through to completion on the day of Christ Jesus.

May 15
Biker George says today is tomorrow that you thought about yesterday & tomorrow is a yesterday that ain't arrived yet.

Ephesians 5:16 (GW) Make the most of your opportunities because these are evil days.

May 16
It seems like many career politicians are like guns without triggers says Biker George. They don't work & can't be fired.

Luke 16:10-12 (GW) Whoever can be trusted with very little can also be trusted with a lot. Whoever is dishonest with very little is dishonest with a lot. Therefore, if you can't be trusted with wealth that is often used dishonestly, who will trust you with wealth that is real? If you can't be trusted with someone else's wealth, who will give you your own?

May 17
God wants our whole heart. Biker George knows God will also accept a broken one, but he wants all the pieces.

Psalm 34:18 (NLT) The Lord is close to the brokenhearted; he rescues those whose spirits are crushed.

May 18
Biker George says we need to keep our heads up & reach for the stars. We might not get one, but we won't get a handful of mud either.

Philippians 3:14 (GW) I run straight toward the goal to win the prize that God's heavenly call offers in Christ Jesus.

May 19
Biker George noticed that some people are always late for church & then they wonder why God seems late in answering their prayers.

Micah 7:7 (KJV) Therefore I will look unto the Lord; I will wait for the God of my salvation: my God will hear me.

May 20
Some say you don't gotta go to church to be a Christian. Biker George compares that to when you jump out of a plane, you don't gotta wear a parachute, but it helps.
Hebrews 10:25 (AMP) not forsaking our meeting together [as believers for worship & instruction], as is the habit of some, but encouraging one another; & all the more [faithfully] as you see the day [of Christ's return] approaching.

May 21
Biker George says you can't run a motorcycle on empty, same as you can't run your life on empty.
John 10:10 (KJV) The thief cometh not, but for to steal, & to kill, & to destroy: I am come that they might have life, & that they might have it more abundantly.

May 22
Biker George says that riding on rough bumpy roads should make us more thankful the smooth ones. Ya know, sometimes we gotta taste the bitter before we can appreciate the sweet.
1 Chronicles 16:34 (KJV) O give thanks unto the Lord; for he is good; for his mercy endureth forever.

May 23
Biker George says that a family altar would alter many a family.
Joshua 24:15 (KJV) ...as for me & my house, we will serve the Lord.

May 24
Biker George says that a true Christian is one who rides right side up in this upside-down world.
Hebrews 2:1 (NLT) So we must listen very carefully to the truth we have heard, or we may drift away from it.

May 25
While it's been said "To err is human, to forgive is divine," Biker George says that sometimes it's "To speed is human, to get caught is a fine."
1 John 1:9 (GW) God is faithful & reliable. If we confess our sins, he forgives them & cleanses us from everything we've done wrong.

May 26
We all have choices to make. Biker George knows God chose us & we choose God!
1 Peter 2:9 (NIRV) But God chose you to be his people. You are royal priests. You are a holy nation. You are a people who belong to God. All of this is so that you can sing his praises. He brought you out of darkness into his wonderful light.

May 27
We are not victims, we are victors in Christ says Biker George.
Romans 8:37 (KJV) ...we are more than conquerors through him that loved us.

May 28
Biker George says some people have a problem riding their bikes because they leave them parked & won't try to start them.
Romans 12:11 (GW) Don't be lazy in showing your devotion. Use your energy to serve the Lord.

May 29
With all the stuff going on in this world, we need to stay in prayer. Biker George says a praying person won't ever be a useless person.
1 Timothy 2:8 (GW) I want men to offer prayers everywhere. They should raise their hands in prayer after putting aside their anger & any quarrels they have with anyone.

May 30
When it comes to prayer, Biker George says don't hang up, hang in there!
Ephesians 6:18 (NLT) Pray in the Spirit at all times & on every occasion. Stay alert & be persistent in your prayers for all believers everywhere.

May 31
Biker George knows some who have prepared for a rainy day, but haven't prepared for eternity.
Luke 12:20-21 (AMP) But God said to him, "You fool! This very night your soul is required of you; & now who will own all the things you have prepared?" So it is for the one who continues to store up & hoard possessions for himself, & is not rich [in his relationship] toward God."

June 1

On the way to a ride, Biker George turned onto a dead-end road by mistake. Ya know that Jesus can turn a hopeless end into endless hope.

Romans 15:13 (NLT) I pray that God, the source of hope, will fill you completely with joy & peace because you trust in him. Then you will overflow with confident hope through the power of the Holy Spirit.

June 2

Forgive us as a nation Lord, prays Biker George.

2 Chronicles 7:14 (KJV) If my people, which are called by my name, shall humble themselves, & pray, & seek my face, & turn from their wicked ways; then will I hear from heaven, & will forgive their sin, & will heal their land.

June 3

If ignorance is bliss, Biker George wonders why ain't more people happy? Ya know ignorance was no excuse when he got caught riding 55 in a 35-mph zone. Not seeing the sign didn't mean anything to the cop & neither will any excuse for not being ready when we meet the Lord.

Mark 1:15 (NLT) "The time promised by God has come at last!" he announced. "The Kingdom of God is near! Repent of your sins & believe the Good News!"

June 4

Biker George says that knowing without doing is like plowing a field without planting the seed.

James 4:17 (KJV) Therefore to him that knoweth to do good, & doeth it not, to him it is sin.

June 5

Biker George asks, do you have a burden for the lost or have you lost the burden? Ya know souls cost soles.

Mark 16:15 (AMP) & He said to them, "Go into all the world & preach the gospel to all creation."

June 6

There's a saying "It's not the destination, it's the ride" which holds true for a lot of rides. However, Biker George says when it comes to our heavenly destination, that is the grand prize for a grand ride!

1 Corinthians 2:9 (NLT) That is what the Scriptures mean when they say, No eye has seen, no ear has heard, & no mind has imagined what God has prepared for those who love him.

June 7

Biker George knows Christ died to save us & lives to keep us. Let's live for Him.

Hebrews 7:25 (NLT) Therefore he is able, once & forever, to save those who come to God through him. He lives forever to intercede with God on their behalf.

Numbers 6:24-26 (NLT) May the Lord bless you & protect you. May the Lord smile on you & be gracious to you. May the Lord show you his favor & give you his peace.

June 8

Ya know, we all need to grow in our faith. Biker George heard it said mile by mile it's a trial, yard by yard it's hard, but inch by inch it's a cinch & faith grows stronger & stronger!

Mark 4:28(NLT) The earth produces the crops on its own. First a leaf blade pushes through, then the heads of wheat are formed, & finally the grain ripens.

June 9

Biker George was thinking of God & thanking God for His love that never fails & never runs out.

Psalm 107:1 (MSG) Oh, thank God - he's so good! His love never runs out.

June 10

Biker George says God is our helper in time of need, so if you worry, you're on your own!

Psalm 54:4 (GW) God is my helper! The Lord is the provider for my life.

June 11

Biker George heard it said that it's easier to get older than it is to get wiser.

Job 8:10 (NLT) But those who came before us will teach you. They will teach you the wisdom of old.

June 12

July 4th is a historical date for our country. Biker George wishes a Happy 4th of July to everyone! Biker Joe still thinks this is the day Will Smith saved us from Aliens.

2 Corinthians 3:17 (AMP) Now the Lord is the Spirit, & where the Spirit of the Lord is, there is liberty [emancipation from bondage, true freedom].

June 13

Biker George woke up & noticed that several neighborhood dogs broke their chains last night. Then he found out that the day after the Fourth of July is one of the busiest for Animal Control. Ya know you don't have till the fireworks to break those chains that bind you. Jesus came to set you free. Call out to Jesus, who is the chain breaker & the way maker!

Psalm 107:13-14 (GW) In their distress they cried out to the Lord. He saved them from their troubles. He brought them out of the dark, out of death's shadow. He broke apart their chains.

June 14

Biker George says that before you can score you gotta have a goal!

Habakkuk 2:2-3 (KJV) & the Lord answered me, & said, Write the vision, & make it plain upon tables, that he may run that readeth it. For the vision is yet for an appointed time, but at the end it shall speak, & not lie: though it tarry, wait for it; because it will surely come, it will not tarry.

June 15

Biker George was riding to a rally he had never been before. Normally he would rather ride all day rather than ask for directions. But then he thought, he doesn't wanna end up like Moses wandering through the desert for 40 years…

Proverbs 12:15 (KJV) The way of a fool is right in his own eyes: but he that hearkeneth unto counsel is wise.

Proverbs 12:15 (MSG) Fools are headstrong & do what they like; wise people take advice.

June 16

Biker George remembers back in his BC (before Christ) days when he was a criminal & then the transformation that took place when he hooked up with Jesus. Ya know, the Lord has a gift of eternal life which is a much better life than we could ever dream of!

John 10:10 (KJV) The thief cometh not, but for to steal, & to kill, & to destroy: I am come that they might have life, & that they might have it more abundantly.

June 17

Biker George remembers years ago laying carpet & losing a pack of cigarettes about the same time. He noticed a lump in the middle of the carpet & figured that he must have dropped them & carpeted over them. Instead of taking up the carpet, he starts to whack the pack with his hammer to flatten them out, so the lump isn't as noticeable. Just at that moment his ole lady walks in the room with his cigarettes in her hand. "You must have left these in the kitchen. Now if only I could find my pet mouse"

James 1:19-20 (NLT) Understand this, my dear brothers & sisters: You must all be quick to listen, slow to speak, & slow to get angry. Human anger does not produce the righteousness God desires.

June 18

Biker George remembers back in the day when he ran track & the main rules were starting, running & finishing. If you think about it, these rules apply to our spiritual lives too. To run a race...ya gotta start & run in the right direction towards the finish line. Never give up, never surrender!

Philippians 3:12-14 (MSG) I'm not saying that I have this all together, that I have it made. But I am well on my way, reaching out for Christ, who has so wondrously reached out for me. Friends, don't get me wrong: By no means do I count myself an expert in all of this, but I've got my eye on the goal, where God is beckoning us onward - to Jesus. I'm off & running, & I'm not turning back.

June 19

Biker George goes to benefit rides as one of the ways to help those in need while remembering that the gift of eternal life is the greatest gift to share. It's the gift that keeps on giving, eternally!

Proverbs 19:17 (MSG) Mercy to the needy is a loan to God, & God pays back those loans in full.

June 20
Biker George went to the mountains & stayed with some real laid-back Hillbillies. One night when everyone was just chillin around the fireplace a conversation went on like this when they thought it was raining. "Get up & go outside & check". "Why don't we just call in the dog & see if he's wet."
Ya know we are so lazy sometimes! We need to be doing more doing & less talking about doing! God wants us to be doers & not just talkers about it. There's so much work to be done!
James 1:22 (KJV) But be ye doers of the word, & not hearers only, deceiving your own selves.

June 21
Biker George noticed people are already preparing their gardens. If you take good care of your garden, it will grow! Ya know, if you take the time to cultivate your spiritual life with God's Word, it will grow!
Isaiah 55:10-11 (NLT) "The rain & snow come down from the heavens & stay on the ground to water the earth. They cause the grain to grow, producing seed for the farmer & bread for the hungry. It is the same with my word. I send it out, & it always produces fruit. It will accomplish all I want it to, & it will prosper everywhere I send it.

June 22
Biker George decided to follow Jesus a while back… He's got a good thing going & he ain't letting go! Be encouraged to hang tight with Jesus!
Psalm 16:8 (NLT) I know the Lord is always with me. I will not be shaken, for he is right beside me.

June 23
Biker George has plans to get a lot of stuff done, but knows that it's God who gives us the ability to do it.
Proverbs 16:9 (NLT) We can make our plans, but the Lord determines our steps.

June 24

Biker Georges says that every day we have choices to make... We can focus on the bad or good... Even in the midst of a storm we can have peace!

Philippians 4:8 (KJV) Finally, brethren, whatsoever things are true, whatsoever things are honest, whatsoever things are just, whatsoever things are pure, whatsoever things are lovely, whatsoever things are of good report; if there be any virtue, & if there be any praise, think on these things.

Psalm 107:29 (NLT) He calmed the storm to a whisper & stilled the waves.

June 25

Biker George went for a long ride to visit his farmer friend. "Watch this!" the farmer said. He gave a whistle & his little dog came running from the house, herded the cattle into the corral, & then latched the gate with her paw. "Wow! That's some dog! What's her name?" The forgetful farmer thought for a minute & then asked "What do you call that red flower that smells good & has thorns on the stem?" "A rose?" "That's it!" The farmer turned to his wife. "Hey Rose, what do we call this dog?

John 14:26 (KJV) But the Comforter, which is the Holy Ghost, whom the Father will send in my name, he shall teach you all things, & bring all things to your remembrance, whatsoever I have said unto you.

Proverbs 10:7 (KJV) The memory of the just is blessed...

June 26

Biker George heard that most accidents happen within two miles of home, so he moved :)

Acts 17:28 (KJV) For in Him we live, & move, & have our being...

2 Corinthians 5:1 (NLT) For we know that when this earthly tent we live in is taken down (that is, when we die & leave this earthly body), we will have a house in heaven, an eternal body made for us by God himself & not by human hands.

June 27

Biker George was thinking about a postage stamp he put on a letter. It sticks to what it's doing through to the end. Ya know, sticking with the Lord will get us through to the end!

Proverbs 18:24 (KJV) A man that hath friends must shew himself friendly: & there is a friend that sticketh closer than a brother.

Matthew 10:22 (KJV) & ye shall be hated of all men for my name's sake: but he that endureth to the end shall be saved.

June 28

Biker George knows that at times life can be hard, but it's even harder if you don't have faith in God.

1 Corinthians 2:5 (KJV) your faith should not stand in the wisdom of men, but in the power of God.

June 29

Biker George has been avoiding junk food & trying to just eat healthy foods that are good for him. End results being good health. What if we all did a spiritual diet to cut out all the bad stuff that we put into our spirit & focus on the Lord & the Word?

Psalm 34:8 (KJV) O taste & see that the Lord is good: blessed is the man that trusteth in him.

Ephesians 4:32 (NLT) Instead, be kind to each other, tenderhearted, forgiving one another, just as God through Christ has forgiven you.

June 30

Biker George has been dealing with allergies & found out that he could plant a lower allergy garden! But while out there planting it, he got bombarded by pollen from oak, maples, grasses & all the others!

Genesis 1:11 (KJV) & God said , Let the earth bring forth grass, the herb yielding seed, & the fruit tree yielding fruit after his kind, whose seed is in itself, upon the earth: & it was so.

JULY

July 1
Biker George remembers when he was a kid & a Sunday School class about how God created everything including Adam & Eve. Later after that class, his mother noticed him lying down like he was sick. She asked, "George, what is the matter?" Little George responded, "I got a pain in my side, I think I'm gonna have a wife!"
Genesis 2:22 (KJV) & the rib, which the Lord God had taken from man, made he a woman, & brought her unto the man.

July 2
Biker George will go just about anywhere to share the Gospel. One day Biker George walked into a bar & went Aaaagh!!! It was an iron bar.
Psalm 32:8 (NLT) The Lord says, "I will guide you along the best pathway for your life. I will advise you & watch over you.

July 3

Biker George knows that we were on His mind when He was on the cross.

1 John 3:16 (NLT) We know what real love is because Jesus gave up his life for us. So we also ought to give up our lives for our brothers & sisters.

July 4

Biker George has seen that the strength of God accompanies the call of God!

1 Peter 5:10 (GW) God, who shows you his kindness & who has called you through Christ Jesus to his eternal glory, will restore you, strengthen you, make you strong, & support you as you suffer for a little while.

July 5

If you're gonna do what you say you're gonna do for the Lord, don't just talk the talk, walk the walk! Or like Biker George says, RIDE THE RIDE!

Short scripture ref: Gal 5:25 (KJV) If we live in the Spirit, let us also walk in the Spirit.

Scripture ref plus: Galatians 5:25-26 (MSG) Since this is the kind of life we have chosen, the life of the Spirit, let us make sure that we do not just hold it as an idea in our heads or a sentiment in our hearts, but work out its implications in every detail of our lives. That means we will not compare ourselves with each other as if one of us were better & another worse. We have far more interesting things to do with our lives. Each of us is an original.

July 6

Biker George remembers a dumb crook that tried to siphon gas from his neighbor's motor home. He caught the poor fool outside of the RV vomiting his guts out. Come to find out, the would-be thief mistakenly put the hose down into the black tank which stores the sewage!

Proverbs 13:20 (NLT) Walk with the wise and become wise; associate with fools and get in trouble.

July 7
Biker George was riding back from a rally doing the posted speed limit when an angry driver in a cage tried to run over him & cussed him out. Funny thing was the car had several "LOVE" bumper stickers on it. Just goes to show that actions speak louder than bumper stickers....

1 John 3:18 (NLT) Dear children, let's not merely say that we love each other; let us show the truth by our actions.

July 8
Biker George says that spiritual correction is not spiritual rejection. It's there to help you, not hurt you.

Proverbs 3:11 (NLT) My child, don't reject the Lord's discipline, & don't be upset when he corrects you.

July 9
Biker George likes to ride fast & says that speed has never killed anyone... It's the suddenly becoming stationary, that gets you.

Romans 13:1 (MSG) Be a good citizen. All governments are under God. In so far as there is peace & order, it's God's order.

July 10
Biker George thinks that somebody should tell Forrest Gump that on the back of boxes of chocolate it tells you what you're gonna get. Reading the Word of God tells you what you gonna get as your eternal reward or punishment.

Matthew 7:13-14 (NLT) You can enter God's Kingdom only through the narrow gate. The highway to hell is broad, & its gate is wide for the many who choose that way. But the gateway to life is very narrow & the road is difficult, & only a few ever find it.

July 11
Biker George used to think he was indecisive, but he ain't too sure.
James 4:8 (KJV) Draw nigh to God, & he will draw nigh to you. Cleanse your hands, ye sinners; & purify your hearts, ye double minded.

July 12
Biker George & Angel were riding in a hurry to get to a benefit ride so he made a right turn at a red light where it said "NO RIGHT TURN ON RED" to save some time. Then it hit him & George said "Oh no... I just made an illegal turn." Angel on the back, leans forward & says "Honey, it's OK... the cop car right behind us just did it too."

James 1:13-14 (NLT) & remember, when you are being tempted, do not say, "God is tempting me." God is never tempted to do wrong, & he never tempts anyone else. Temptation comes from our own desires, which entice us & drag us away.

July 13
To Biker George's ole lady an "All Nighter" now means not getting up to pee!

2 Corinthians 4:16-18 (MSG) 16-18 So we're not giving up. How could we! Even though on the outside it often looks like things are falling apart on us, on the inside, where God is making new life, not a day goes by without his unfolding grace. These hard times are small potatoes compared to the coming good times, the lavish celebration prepared for us. There's far more here than meets the eye. The things we see now are here today, gone tomorrow. But the things we can't see now will last forever.

July 14
Biker George only prays on days that end with the letter "y".

Romans 12:12 (NLT) Rejoice in our confident hope. Be patient in trouble, & keep on praying.

July 15
Biker George says some witnessing is better than no witnessing because you are being obedient to Christ's command. Practice makes perfect. We all had to crawl before we learned to walk.

Matthew 9:37-38 (KJV) Then saith he unto his disciples, The harvest truly is plenteous, but the labourers are few; Pray ye therefore the Lord of the harvest, that he will send forth labourers into his harvest.

July 16

Biker George remembers hearing it said in the movie God's Not Dead, that sometimes the devil allows people to live a life free of trouble because he doesn't want them turning to God. Their sin is like a jail cell, except it is all nice & comfy & there doesn't seem to be any reason to leave. The door's wide open. Till one day, time runs out, & the cell door slams shut, & suddenly it's too late.

Romans 6:20-23 (MSG) As long as you did what you felt like doing, ignoring God, you didn't have to bother with right thinking or right living, or right anything for that matter. But do you call that a free life? What did you get out of it? Nothing you're proud of now. Where did it get you? A dead end. But now that you've found you don't have to listen to sin tell you what to do, & have discovered the delight of listening to God telling you, what a surprise! A whole, healed, put-together life right now, with more & more of life on the way! Work hard for sin your whole life & your pension is death. But God's gift is real life, eternal life, delivered by Jesus, our Master.

July 17

Biker George says it's a great ride when we travel the road together in the same direction.

Ephesians 4:4 (AMP) There is one body [of believers] & one Spirit - just as you were called to one hope when called [to salvation]

July 18

Biker George says that part of our purpose here on earth is to shine as lights, not get used to the dark.

Matthew 5:13-16 (NLT) "You are the salt of the earth. But what good is salt if it has lost its flavor? Can you make it salty again? It will be thrown out & trampled underfoot as worthless. You are the light of the world - like a city on a hilltop that cannot be hidden. No one lights a lamp & then puts it under a basket. Instead, a lamp is placed on a stand, where it gives light to everyone in the house. In the same way, let your good deeds shine out for all to see, so that everyone will praise your heavenly Father.

July 19
Biker George was having a coffee at the Greasy Spoon & saw a blind guy walk in with a white cane. The man had his hand on his friend's shoulder which he trusted to lead him. A good leader knows the way, shows the way, & goes the way. Follow Jesus.

Proverbs 29:2 (KJV) When the righteous are in authority, the people rejoice: but when the wicked beareth rule, the people mourn.

July 20
Biker George says, We are a victors in Christ, not victims!

1 Corinthians 15:57 (KJV) But thanks be to God, which giveth us the victory through our Lord Jesus Christ.

July 21
Biker George says that telling someone you care is one thing. But showing you care is what counts.

Ephesians 4:32 (NLT) Instead, be kind to each other, tenderhearted, forgiving one another, just as God through Christ has forgiven you.

July 22
Biker George says, Give God your life, He can do more with it than you can.

Romans 6:13 (NLT) Do not let any part of your body become an instrument of evil to serve sin. Instead, give yourselves completely to God, for you were dead, but now you have new life. So use your whole body as an instrument to do what is right for the glory of God.

July 23
Biker George remembers when he was a little kid & his Daddy built him a tree house in the woods near his house. The woods were so thick that George didn't really feel safe until Daddy made a path so he could see the house. Sometimes we might wish our Daddy God would make a trail for us through the thick woods of the future like He did for Israel as they left Egypt. When the path ain't clear we need to remember, follow the Holy Spirit's leading & God's Word.

Psalm 31:3 (KJV) For thou art my rock & my fortress; therefore for thy name's sake lead me, & guide me.

July 24

Biker George is having some fruit for breakfast. What kinda fruit do you got? Not talking about the breakfast bar. Do you got the fruit of the spirit?

Galatians 5:22-26 (NLT) But the Holy Spirit produces this kind of fruit in our lives: love, joy, peace, patience, kindness, goodness, faithfulness, gentleness, & self-control. There is no law against these things! Those who belong to Christ Jesus have nailed the passions & desires of their sinful nature to his cross & crucified them there. Since we are living by the Spirit, let us follow the Spirit's leading in every part of our lives. Let us not become conceited, or provoke one another, or be jealous of one another.

July 25

Biker George has a choice on which path to take in life, just as we all do. If we follow the Lord's will He will show which path to take.

Proverbs 3:5-6 (NLT) Trust in the lord with all your heart; do not depend on your own understanding. Seek his will in all you do, & he will show you which path to take.

July 26

Biker George says strong trials build strong faith. You can let it make you better or bitter. Putting your cares on Jesus can be a great stress reliever!

In John 14:1 (NLT) Jesus said...Don't let your hearts be troubled. Trust in God, & trust also in me.

July 27

Our life here on earth isn't the end, it's the beginning of eternity. Where will you spend it?

2 Peter 3:8 (KJV) But, beloved, be not ignorant of this one thing, that one day is with the Lord as a thousand years, & a thousand years as one day.

July 28

Biker George heard it once said that you can tell you're getting old when you got more candles on the cake than friends at the birthday party.

Proverbs 9:11 (KJV) For by me thy days shall be multiplied, & the years of thy life shall be increased.

July 29

Biker George says that nobody has ever got poor by giving to others. If you feel the Lord is nudging you to help others, check out BikerDownLiftedUp.org, a 501(c)(3) non-profit organization that has been helping bikers since 2009. The mission of this motorcycle ministry is dedicated to lifting up downed bikers through prayer & financial assistance.

Proverbs 24:11 (MSG) Rescue the perishing; don't hesitate to step in & help.

July 30

Biker George doesn't really care for Mondays. But to get to Friday we have to go through the Mondays!

Isaiah 40:31 (KJV) But they that wait upon the LORD shall renew their strength; they shall mount up with wings as eagles; they shall run, & not be weary; & they shall walk, & not faint.

Romans 6:13 (NLT) Do not let any part of your body become an instrument of evil to serve sin. Instead, give yourselves completely to God, for you were dead, but now you have new life. So use your whole body as an instrument to do what is right for the glory of God.

July 31

Biker George is a hardcore biker. He loves his motorcycle. However, George would lay down his motorcycle to be with his ole lady. After all Jesus loved us so much that He laid down His life for us.

Ephesians 5:25 (KJV) Husbands, love your wives, even as Christ also loved the church, & gave himself for it.

August 1

Biker George's ole lady, Angel asked "How did everything get so dirty so fast I cleaned the whole house a month ago." George replied "Cleaning is a way of life, not a once a month thing, because speck by speck, dust returns & piece by piece, the clutter piles up." You know, sin can be like dust & clutter in a house. Confession & repentance need to be a way of life, not a once a month thing!

1 John 1:9 (KJV) If we confess our sins, he is faithful & just to forgive us our sins, & to cleanse us from all unrighteousness.

August 2

Biker George has learned that sometimes our good decisions come from bad experiences, which sometimes came from our bad decisions.

Proverbs 1:5 (KJV) A wise man will hear, and will increase learning; and a man of understanding shall attain unto wise counsels:

August 3

People come from all over the world to Sturgis, SD for the huge motorcycle rally in August. Biker George says that sharing the Gospel in Sturgis is like being on a different overseas mission trip every day! Remember the mission field first starts in your back yard & community, and then it goes out from there.

Romans 10:13-14 (NLT) For "Everyone who calls on the name of the Lord will be saved." But how can they call on him to save them unless they believe in him? And how can they believe in him if they have never heard about him? And how can they hear about him unless someone tells them?

August 4

Biker George says that hitting rock bottom is hard but sometimes that's what it takes to draw some closer or back to the Lord. When a Christian hits rock bottom, they find that Jesus is the firm foundation!

Psalm 119:71 (NLT) My suffering was good for me, for it taught me to pay attention to your decrees.

August 5

Biker George sometime feels like "Bandit". He's gonna do what they say can't be done. He's got a long way to go & a short time to get there it seems. As long as you are running towards the Lord & He is on your side, you're gonna get the job done!

Psalm 50:15 (NLT) Then call on me when you are in trouble, & I will rescue you, & you will give me glory."

August 6

God does not ask us to go where he does not lead. Place your hand in His hand, and let Him lead the way.

Psalm 32:8 (KJV) I will instruct thee and teach thee in the way which thou shalt go: I will guide thee with mine eye.

August 7

Biker George has seen dogs that bark at strangers. sorta like when some will avoid bikers at all cost & those who avoid knowing Jesus. Get to know a biker & better yet... get to know Jesus.

John 7:24 (KJV) Judge not according to the appearance, but judge righteous judgment.

August 8

One day at a rally Biker George & Angel overheard a guy ask, "Does anyone know where this line is going?" The guy next to him said, "I ain't got a clue." George laughed quietly at this, but then realized that he didn't know where it was going either. It didn't matter though... George & Angel were holding hands & having a good time. It wasn't important where they were going... It was being together that mattered most. We might not know where life's road will take us, but we can enjoy the journey if we are walking with our Lord!

Colossians 2:6 (KJV) As ye have therefore received Christ Jesus the Lord, so walk ye in him

August 9

Biker George asks why can't you forgive some people? Did they beat you to a bloody pulp, whip your back 39 times until it looked like shredded meat, pull your beard out, & crucify you on a cross? If Jesus can forgive those who crucified Him why can't we forgive others?

Matthew 6:15 (NLT) But if you refuse to forgive others, your Father will not forgive your sins.

August 10

Biker George heard it once said that you can tell you're getting old when you got more candles on the cake than friends at the birthday party.

Proverbs 9:11 (KJV) For by me thy days shall be multiplied, & the years of thy life shall be increased.

August 11

Biker George says that opinions can be a dime a dozen, but the Word of the Lord is priceless!

2 Timothy 3:16-17 (NLT) All Scripture is inspired by God & is useful to teach us what is true & to make us realize what is wrong in our lives. It corrects us when we are wrong & teaches us to do what is right. God uses it to prepare & equip his people to do every good work.

August 12
Biker George has been avoiding junk food & trying to just eat healthy foods that are good for him. End results being good health. What if we all did a spiritual diet to cut out all the bad stuff that we put into our spirit & focus on the Lord & the Word?
Psalm 34:8 (KJV) O taste & see that the Lord is good: blessed is the man that trusteth in him.

August 13
Biker George says that since we are the church, then the rapture would be separation of church & state :)
1 Thessalonians 4:17 (NLT) Then, together with them, we who are still alive & remain on the earth will be caught up in the clouds to meet the Lord in the air. Then we will be with the Lord forever.

August 14
Biker George says that even though the world may discount you, in God's eyes you are priceless & that's what counts!
Zechariah 2:8 (AMP) For thus says the Lord of hosts, "After glory He has sent Me against the nations which plunder you - for he who touches you, touches the apple of His eye.

August 15
We need to reach the lost at any cost! Ya know, Jesus paid the cost so we could reach the lost, so let's get out there & share the Gospel!
Acts 1:8 (NLT) But you will receive power when the Holy Spirit comes upon you. And you will be my witnesses, telling people about me everywhere - in Jerusalem, throughout Judea, in Samaria, & to the ends of the earth."

August 16
Biker George is a hardcore biker. He loves his motorcycle. However, George would lay down his motorcycle to be with his ole lady. After all Jesus loved us so much that He laid down His life for us.
Ephesians 5:25 (KJV) Husbands, love your wives, even as Christ also loved the church, & gave himself for it

August 17
Biker George says to all of those who are serving in God's army as secret service agents. Stop keeping the faith! Spread it around!
Matthew 5:15 (NLT) No one lights a lamp & then puts it under a basket. Instead, a lamp is placed on a stand, where it gives light to everyone in the house.

August 18
Biker George just had a thought... While hand sanitizer can wash away the flu & cold germs from our hands, the blood of Jesus can wash away our sins!
Isaiah 1:18 (NLT) "Come now, let's settle this," says the Lord. "Though your sins are like scarlet, I will make them as white as snow. Though they are red like crimson, I will make them as white as wool.

August 19
Biker George was praying... Lord, today I've done good so far. I haven't been mean, got mad, or anything bad, but I'm fixin' to get out of bed & I'm probably gonna need a lot of help. In Jesus name, Amen.
Isaiah 41:10 (NLT) Don't be afraid, for I am with you. Don't be discouraged, for I am your God. I will strengthen you & help you. I will hold you up with my victorious right hand

August 20
Biker George says that putting Jesus to be first in your marriage can help your marriage to last. Got Jesus in your marriage?
Ecclesiastes 4:12 (KJV) & if one prevail against him, two shall withstand him; & a threefold cord is not quickly broken.

August 21
Biker George sometime feels like "Bandit". He's gonna do what they say can't be done. He's got a long way to go & a short time to get there it seems. As long as you are running towards the Lord & He is on your side, you're gonna get the job done!
Psalm 50:15 (NLT) Then call on me when you are in trouble, & I will rescue you, & you will give me glory."

August 22
Biker George says that no matter how it looks & even if it looks like you got nothing left, you still got prayer...and that's enough!
Deuteronomy 31:8 (NLT) Do not be afraid or discouraged, for the Lord will personally go ahead of you. He will be with you; he will neither fail you nor abandon you."

August 23
Biker George has seen dogs that bark at strangers. sorta like when some will avoid bikers at all cost & those who avoid knowing Jesus. Get to know a biker & better yet... get to know Jesus.
John 7:24 (KJV) Judge not according to the appearance, but judge righteous judgment.

August 24
Biker George says that since we are the church, the rapture would be separation of church & state.
1 Thessalonians 4:17 (NLT) Then, together with them, we who are still alive & remain on the earth will be caught up in the clouds to meet the Lord in the air. Then we will be with the Lord forever.

August 25
Biker George asks why can't you forgive some people? Did they beat you to a bloody pulp, whip your back 39 times until it looked like shredded meat, pull your beard out, & crucify you on a cross? If Jesus can forgive those who crucified Him why can't we forgive others?
Matthew 6:15 (NLT) But if you refuse to forgive others, your Father will not forgive your sins.

August 26
Biker George was watching an artist as he painted a picture. George asked "Why do you put all of those amazing colors into your pictures? I never see anything like that in nature." The artist replied "Don't you wish you did?" Ya know... God paints better than Pablo Picasso or any other artist. Look at the skies, the mountains, the oceans, the universe!!! My God, how great thou art!
Ephesians 2:10 (KJV) For we are his workmanship, created in Christ Jesus unto good works, which God hath before ordained that we should walk in them.

August 27

We shouldn't waste our breath arguing about how to worship. There are many ways to worship God, but only one God to worship! Psalm 150:6 (KJV) Let everything that hath breath praise the LORD. Praise ye the LORD.

August 28

Biker George says that it's good to learn from past mistakes, but it's not good to live in the past.

Lamentations 3:22-23 (NLT) The faithful love of the Lord never ends! His mercies never cease. Great is his faithfulness; his mercies begin afresh each morning.

August 29

Biker has noticed that messages that convict people of sin in their life are sometimes as welcome as a thunderstorm during a ride. When you get a chance read Jeremiah 26.

Galatians 6:1 (NLT) Dear brothers & sisters, if another believer is overcome by some sin, you who are godly should gently & humbly help that person back onto the right path. And be careful not to fall into the same temptation yourself.

August 30

Biker George was getting his scoot fixed at the shop. He knew this would have been big bucks if not for the warranty. Then the mechanic came in & said, "The warranty has expired. I will have to charge you & it ain't gonna be cheap." Isn't it good to know that God's promises never expire & are always under warranty!

Hebrews 13:5 (KJV) I will never leave thee, nor forsake thee.

Acts 1:8 (NLT) But you will receive power when the Holy Spirit comes upon you. And you will be my witnesses, telling people about me everywhere - in Jerusalem, throughout Judea, in Samaria, & to the ends of the earth."

SEPTEMBER

September 1

Biker George knows that we need to make allowances for each other's faults, & forgive anyone who offends us. Remembering that the Lord forgave us, so we must forgive others. George smiled as he overheard a youngster reciting the Lord's Prayer at a church "And forgive us our trash passes, as we forgive those who passed trash against us."

Matthew 6:14-15 (NLT) "If you forgive those who sin against you, your heavenly Father will forgive you. But if you refuse to forgive others, your Father will not forgive your sins."

September 2

Biker George says you don't find friends. You make them.

Proverbs 17:17 (NLT) A friend is always loyal, & a brother is born to help in time of need.

September 3

How can people say they are a biker if they don't know anything about motorcycles, or even associate with bikers? How can people say they are a Christian but they don't know Jesus Christ or associate with Christians? Biker George says the perfect answer to these questions & more is to get out & ride to church!

Hebrews 10:25 (NLT) & let us not neglect our meeting together, as some people do, but encourage one another, especially now that the day of his return is drawing near.

September 4

Biker George had this city friend who always slept in as long as he could. One morning he got up even later than usual & was late for work. He hurried up, got dressed & ran out the door & jumped on the city bus as it was pulling out & then asked where's this bus going?

Where's your life going? Are you headed in the right direction? A lot of people are making good time, but they're going the wrong way.

Psalm 25:4-5 (NLT) Show me the right path, O Lord; point out the road for me to follow. Lead me by your truth and teach me, for you are the God who saves me. All day long I put my hope in you.

September 5

Biker George remembers when he was a kid being taught that the world is spinning so fast that a person standing on the equator is rotating with the earth at 1,000 MPH. It doesn't seem like we are moving at all but appearances can be deceiving. George also remembers being taught that Jesus will return as He promised. To some it may appear like He ain't gonna come back, but appearances can be deceiving because Jesus' second coming is as certain as His first coming!

2 Peter 3:3-4 (NLT) Most importantly, I want to remind you that in the last days scoffers will come, mocking the truth & following their own desires. They will say, "What happened to the promise that Jesus is coming again? From before the times of our ancestors, everything has remained the same since the world was first created."

September 6

Biker George noticed the cows in the field are always chewing their cud which means they are happy & healthy. To be a spiritually healthy Christian we need to chew the cud more & not treat the Bible as snack food.

Psalm 1:2 (MSG) ...you thrill to God's Word, you chew on Scripture day & night.

September 7

Heard tell that years ago Pepper Rodgers was in the midst of a terrible football season as coach at UCLA. It even got so bad that it upset his home life. He recalled that his dog was his only friend & told his wife that a man needs at least two friends. So, she bought him another dog!

Romans 12:10 (NLT) Love each other with genuine affection, & take delight in honoring each other.

September 8

We've all heard the old saying "Those who don't learn from history are bound to repeat it". Well, ya know the Bible has a lot of history of people who made mistakes that we can learn from. We can ask the Lord to protect us from making similar mistakes.

Psalm 119:11 (KJV) Thy word have I hid in mine heart, that I might not sin against thee.

September 9

Biker George woke up this morning & really just wanted to sleep in. But ya know, this day will only last for a day & it is special. God made it, & as we get out there & show others the joy of the Lord, it may impact their life eternally! So, get your motor running, head out on the highway, be looking for adventure!

Psalm 118:24 (KJV) This is the day which the Lord hath made; we will rejoice & be glad in it.

Matthew 6:14-15 (NLT) "If you forgive those who sin against you, your heavenly Father will forgive you. But if you refuse to forgive others, your Father will not forgive your sins."

September 10
While some may say "Live to Ride, Ride to Live" Biker George has been known to say "He Died For us, I Ride For Him". Ya know, Jesus Christ died on the cross for our sins so that is why we ride to spread the Gospel.

Acts 17:28 (NLT) For in him we live & move & exist. As some of your own poets have said, "We are his offspring."

September 11
Biker George can relate to peace beyond all understanding & the saying. Know God: Know peace. No God: No peace.

John 14:27 (KJV) Peace I leave with you, my peace I give unto you: not as the world giveth, give I unto you. Let not your heart be troubled, neither let it be afraid.

September 12
How many times do we try to figure everything out on our own when we should be trusting God from the bottom of our heart. Ya know if we listen for God's voice He will keep us on track.

Proverbs 3:5-6 (KJV) Trust in the Lord with all thine heart; & lean not unto thine own understanding. In all thy ways acknowledge him, & he shall direct thy paths.

September 13
If you found a cure for cancer, you would share it with the world, right? What about sharing the Gospel with those who don't know that they can have sins forgiven & be able to look forward to eternity in Heaven? Biker George says, don't keep the gift of life to yourself!

Romans 10:13-15 (NLT) For "Everyone who calls on the name of the Lord will be saved." But how can they call on him to save them unless they believe in him? & how can they believe in him if they have never heard about him? & how can they hear about him unless someone tells them? & how will anyone go & tell them without being sent?

Proverbs 14:25 (KJV) A true witness delivereth souls: but a deceitful witness speaketh lies.

September 14

Do the math... sin adds to your troubles, subtracts from your energy, multiplies your difficulties, & divides you from God. Biker George has the answer book for this math problem & that book is the Bible.

1 John 1:6-7 (NLT) So we are lying if we say we have fellowship with God but go on living in spiritual darkness; we are not practicing the truth. But if we are living in the light, as God is in the light, then we have fellowship with each other, & the blood of Jesus, his Son, cleanses us from all sin.

September 15

Biker George has been to several great Christian Concerts. He has seen many lives changed because of Christian music. There is one concert of the ages coming that Jesus paid the price for the ticket! When the last trumpet is blown you want to be ready!

1 Corinthians 15:51-53 (NLT) But let me reveal to you a wonderful secret. We will not all die, but we will all be transformed! It will happen in a moment, in the blink of an eye, when the last trumpet is blown. For when the trumpet sounds, those who have died will be raised to live forever. And we who are living will also be transformed. For our dying bodies must be transformed into bodies that will never die; our mortal bodies must be transformed into immortal bodies.

September 16

Biker George thanks God for all of the people who have been saved from the floods and the hurricanes. But there is coming an even more epic event that will wreak havoc on the world. Are you ready for eternity?

Acts 2:21 (KJV) And it shall come to pass, that whosoever shall call on the name of the Lord shall be saved.

September 17

Biker George was rejoicing when he heard that five of his club members got saved & baptized! Then come the good news/bad news. Good news: All five were baptized in the river. Bad news: Two of them got swept away by the rapids.

Proverbs 15:30 (NLT) A cheerful look brings joy to the heart; good news makes for good health.

Acts 17:28 (NLT) For in him we live & move & exist. As some of your own poets have said, "We are his offspring.

September 18

Biker George says "Get into the Bible & let the Bible get into you!"

Colossians 3:16 (KJV) Let the word of Christ dwell in you richly...

Philippians 4:13 (KJV) I can do all things through Christ which strengtheneth me.

September 19

Biker George was down on his luck & praying for some food. He then looked out on his porch & there were bags of groceries! He shouts "PRAISE THE LORD!" His atheist neighbor shouts back, "There is no God, I bought those groceries!" That made George even more excited! "PRAISE THE LORD! He not only sent me groceries, but He made the devil pay for them!"

Proverbs 3:5 (NLT) Trust in the LORD with all your heart; do not depend on your own understanding.

September 20

Biker George says that before you score you must have a goal. Keeping some good spiritual goals ahead of you can help you score some spiritual growth. Just a few ideas like reading the Bible daily & getting to know Jesus better can impact you & others to make an eternal difference in the lives of many.

2 Peter 3:18 (KJV) But grow in grace, & in the knowledge of our Lord & Saviour Jesus Christ...

September 21

Biker George knows the quote about insanity is doing the same thing over & over again & expecting different results. Hook up with Jesus & the results will be fruitful. Without Him is insanity!

John 15:5 (NLT) "Yes, I am the vine; you are the branches. Those who remain in me, & I in them, will produce much fruit. For apart from me you can do nothing.

September 22

Biker George was just thinking of the song, Jesus loves me this I know…. If you know this, it's time to share some of that love with others. If you don't know about the love of Jesus, check out the Bible. He's got a FREE gift that lasts for eternity!

Romans 5:8 (NLT) But God showed his great love for us by sending Christ to die for us while we were still sinners.

September 23

Biker George has noticed church people have various opinions about music. For some Christians it's gotta be what's playing on the Christian radio station, some want the old hymns, some want a rock concert, some want a full orchestra, some fold their arms, some clap, some raise their hands, & some focus on worshiping the Lord & realize that Praise & Worship leads us into worship of the one who is worthy to be praised. Ya know, we shouldn't waste our breath arguing about how to worship. There are many ways to worship God, but only one God to worship!

Psalm 150:6 (KJV) Let every thing that hath breath praise the LORD. Praise ye the LORD.

September 24

Biker George heard it once said that you don't stop laughing because you grow old. You grow old because you stopped laughing.

Proverbs 17:22 (NLT) A cheerful heart is good medicine, but a broken spirit saps a person's strength.

Psalm 42:1-2 (KJV) As the hart panteth after the water brooks, so panteth my soul after thee, O God. My soul thirsteth for God, for the living God: when shall I come & appear before God?

September 25
Biker George was thinking. We have choices to make. We can decide to follow Jesus & be blessed as we trust in Him & taste of His goodness. Or the opposite.... Either way, God is good, but you got to accept that FREE gift of salvation & trust in Him!
Psalm 34:8 (KJV) O taste & see that the LORD is good: blessed is the man that trusteth in him.

September 26
Biker George was cleaning the bugs off of his bike's windshield when it occurred to him that some days it's like he's the bug, & on some days he is the windshield.
1 John 4:4 (KJV) ...greater is he that is in you, than he that is in the world!

September 27
Biker George remembers as kid growing up with a black & white TV that had really bad reception. But none the less little George was glad his family had a TV. One day his dad found out he needed to connect it to the roof-top antenna & the TV started coming in crystal clear! George never forgot that day! Life with no relationship with God through Jesus Christ is like that TV without an antenna! Have you seen Jesus clearly in God's Word? Are you helping others to see Him clearly too?
Mark 8:25 (NLT) Then Jesus placed his hands on the man's eyes again, & his eyes were opened. His sight was completely restored, & he could see everything clearly.

September 28
As you go out into the highways to share the Gospel, the Lord will bless you with witnessing opportunities! Be believing that the seeds sown will produce a great harvest in the appointed time!
2 Corinthians 9:10 (NLT) For God is the one who provides seed for the farmer & then bread to eat. In the same way, he will provide & increase your resources & then produce a great harvest of generosity in you.
Philippians 4:13 (KJV) I can do all things through Christ which strengtheneth me.

September 29

Biker George says that people who think they don't need God are in a no win situation for this journey of life. Instead of falling away from God, fall into His arms! Take time to humble yourself before God & with His strength you can do it!

Philippians 3:14 (NLT) I press on to reach the end of the race & receive the heavenly prize for which God, through Christ Jesus, is calling us.

Jude 1:24 (NLT) Now all glory to God, who is able to keep you from falling away & will bring you with great joy into his glorious presence without a single fault.

September 30

Biker George says, To walk with God, you must talk with God. There is no need to fear where you're going if God is going with you!

Deuteronomy 31:8 (NLT) Do not be afraid or discouraged, for the LORD will personally go ahead of you. He will be with you; he will neither fail you nor abandon you.

October 1
Biker George got some antibiotics from the doctor. Reading the bottle is a good thing to do, but he needs to take them for real change to take place. This is sorta like the Word of God... You can read the Bible, but you gotta get it down inside of you for real change to take place!
Colossians 3:16 (KJV) Let the word of Christ dwell in you richly...
1 John 4:4 (KJV) ...greater is he that is in you, than he that is in the world.

October 2
Biker George knows that you don't have to be a person of influence to be an influence on others. Be a good example in whatever you do.
Colossians 3:17 (KJV) And whatsoever ye do in word or deed, do all in the name of the Lord Jesus, giving thanks to God and the Father by him.

October 3

Biker George has learned not to let unjust criticism about him or the ministry get him down. What God knows about us is more important than what people think or say about us.

1 Samuel 16:7 (KJV) ...man looketh on the outward appearance, but the Lord looketh on the heart.

Matthew 5:11 (KJV) Blessed are ye, when men shall revile you, & persecute you, & shall say all manner of evil against you falsely, for my sake.

October 4

Biker George says "Don't let life happen to you. Let life happen through you!" Instead of dodging life's bullets, maybe we can be a fountain of blessing to others by allowing God to work through us. Are you a target or a fountain? God blesses us to bless others!

Deuteronomy 30:19 (NLT) Today I have given you the choice between life & death, between blessings & curses. Now I call on heaven & earth to witness the choice you make. Oh, that you would choose life, so that you & your descendants might live!

October 5

As we go out into the highways to share the Gospel, the Lord continues to bless us with witnessing opportunities! We are believing that the seeds sown will produce a great harvest in the appointed time!

2 Corinthians 9:10 (NLT) For God is the one who provides seed for the farmer & then bread to eat. In the same way, he will provide & increase your resources & then produce a great harvest of generosity in you.

October 6

Biker George use to speed read through the Bible to cover as many pages as he could instead of letting God's Word cover him. Instead of quality he was looking for quantity. Some of it did sink in, but we really need to read & study the Bible more as if God were speaking to us through His Word, because He is!

1 Peter 2:2 (KJV) As newborn babes, desire the sincere milk of the word, that ye may grow thereby

October 7

Biker George remembers as kid growing up with a black & white TV that had really bad reception. But none the less little George was glad his family had a TV. One day his dad found out he needed to connect it to the roof-top antenna & the TV started coming in crystal clear! George never forgot that day! Life with no relationship with God through Jesus Christ is like that TV without an antenna! Have you seen Jesus clearly in God's Word? Are you helping others to see Him clearly too?

Mark 8:25 (NLT) Then Jesus placed his hands on the man's eyes again, & his eyes were opened. His sight was completely restored, & he could see everything clearly.

October 8

Biker George was wondering why some people can't seem to accept God's forgiveness. God keeps His word & if we ask Him to forgive us, He forgives us. Ya know, when God forgives we can forget about it! He does!

1 John 1:9 (KJV) If we confess our sins, he is faithful & just to forgive us our sins, & to cleanse us from all unrighteousness.

Hebrews 8:12 (KJV) For I will be merciful to their unrighteousness, & their sins & their iniquities will I remember no more.

October 9

Biker George was on a train & heard a little girl shout at her mom that the train is going to run into a mountain! In a few seconds a tunnel let the train pass through. Then the little girl said "Someone must have gone before us & made a way for us." Ya know...We can go through anything because Jesus goes before us.

Deuteronomy 31:6 (NLT) So be strong & courageous! Do not be afraid & do not panic before them. For the Lord your God will personally go ahead of you. He will neither fail you nor abandon you."

October 10

Biker George says that there are a bunch of needs everywhere to be praying for. Sometimes the hard part is following through on our commitment to pray. We may need to remind ourselves throughout the day that we have a job to do. People are counting on us. Ya know that praying frequently will lead to praying fervently!

James 5:16 (KJV) ...The effectual fervent prayer of a righteous man availeth much.

October 11

Biker George says that in the grand scheme of things that our lives are like dust in the wind. We could live to be 100+ years old on this earth & that is just a drop in the bucket compared to the ocean of eternity. Without Christ we're not ready to die, but with Christ we have every reason to live.

James 4:14 (NLT) How do you know what your life will be like tomorrow? Your life is like the morning fog, it's here a little while, then it's gone.

Jude 1:24 (NLT) Now all glory to God, who is able to keep you from falling away & will bring you with great joy into his glorious presence without a single fault.

October 12

Biker George says that it's more important that the character inside of you is bigger than your outside character. A race car with a weed eater engine ain't gonna get it.

1 John 4:4 (NLT) But you belong to God, my dear children. You have already won a victory over those people, because the Spirit who lives in you is greater than the spirit who lives in the world.

Colossians 3:16 (KJV) Let the word of Christ dwell in you richly...

1 John 4:4 (KJV) ...greater is he that is in you, than he that is in the world.

October 13

Biker George is on a passenger train that's creeping along when it finally it creaks to a halt. George asks the conductor "What's going on?" "Cow on the track!" replies the conductor. Ten minutes later, the train resumes it's slow pace. But within five minutes, it stops again. George & leans out the window & yells to the conductor walking down the track, "What happened? Did we catch up with the cow again?"

Philippians 3:14 (NLT) I press on to reach the end of the race & receive the heavenly prize for which God, through Christ Jesus, is calling us.

October 14

Biker George was told the Great Commission wasn't a "stay at home" project because you can't catch any fish unless you go fishing in the water. Note that with the increase in social media we can do "some" fishing from home, but there are some big ones out there that actually may require you to get wet & work up a sweat!

Matthew 28:19-20 (NLT) Therefore, go & make disciples of all the nations, baptizing them in the name of the Father & the Son & the Holy Spirit. Teach these new disciples to obey all the commands I have given you. And be sure of this: I am with you always, even to the end of the age."

October 15

Biker George says we should keep every promise we make & only make promises we can keep. We need to learn not to take it personally when someone keeps saying they'll do something & it doesn't happen.

Ecclesiastes 5:5 (NLT) It is better to say nothing than to make a promise & not keep it.

October 16

Biker George says, God has some good plans for our lives! Let's not mess it up & try to do it our way!

Jeremiah 29:11 (NLT) "For I know the plans I have for you," says the Lord. "They are plans for good & not for disaster, to give you a future & a hope."

October 17

Biker George & his ole lady, Angel were fussing. George told Angel that he had been praying for their relationship to get better. "Thanks", said Angel, "If you ask God to help you not to fuss, He will help you." "Oh, I didn't ask Him that," said George. "I asked Him to help you put up with me." Ya know in prayer, God hears more than the words. He listens to your heart.

Philippians 4:6-7 (NLT) Don't worry about anything; instead, pray about everything. Tell God what you need, & thank him for all he has done. Then you will experience God's peace, which exceeds anything we can understand. His peace will guard your hearts & minds as you live in Christ Jesus.

1 Peter 2:2 (KJV) As newborn babes, desire the sincere milk of the word, that ye may grow thereby.

October 18

Biker George has noticed some of the smartest people do the stupidest things. For example, Ben Franklin nearly killed himself giving an electric shock to a turkey or Richard Feynman, in preparation for a stay in Brazil, studied Spanish. Some people heading into eternity may be even more shortsighted. The one who lives for this life only will have eternity to regret it.

Matthew 16:26 (NLT) & what do you benefit if you gain the whole world but lose your own soul?

Deuteronomy 31:6 (NLT) So be strong & courageous! Do not be afraid & do not panic before them. For the Lord your God will personally go ahead of you. He will neither fail you nor abandon you."

October 19

Biker George remembers when he was a kid he couldn't wait to grow up. Now that he's older & has some health problems, he misses the days of his youth! No matter what season of life you are in, spring, summer, fall or winter...if you have Jesus in your heart, the best is yet to come!

2 Corinthians 4:17-18 (NLT) For our present troubles are small & won't last very long. Yet they produce for us a glory that vastly outweighs them & will last forever! So, we don't look at the troubles we can see now; rather, we fix our gaze on things that cannot be seen. For the things we see now will soon be gone, but the things we cannot see will last forever.

James 5:16 (KJV) ...The effectual fervent prayer of a righteous man availeth much.

October 20

Winners, losers, wealthy, or poor... Jesus paid the price for all. Those who choose to accept the free gift of salvation are the real winners no matter how it looks!

1 Corinthians 6:20 (KJV) For ye are bought with a price: therefore glorify God in your body, & in your spirit, which are God's.

James 4:14 (NLT) How do you know what your life will be like tomorrow? Your life is like the morning fog, it's here a little while, then it's gone.

October 21

Biker George heard that back in the 1700's Ben Franklin set a good example for others by placing a lantern outside his home. The pitch-black streets had rocks & holes that people would stumble across in the night until they passed by Ben's house where the light was shining. Others started putting up lanterns & eventually the whole village was lit up!

Sometimes it's a dark world out there... Let Christ shine through you!

Matthew 5:16 (KJV) Let your light so shine before men, that they may see your good works, & glorify your Father which is in heaven.

October 22

Biker George once said "To get more of the Lord we need less of us."

John 3:30 (KJV) He must increase, but I must decrease.

October 23

Biker George noticed that about everyday he has an opportunity to get angry, stressed or offended. You can choose not to let the little things upset you, but instead let the joy of the Lord be your strength!

Colossians 3:13 (NLT) Make allowance for each other's faults, & forgive anyone who offends you. Remember, the Lord forgave you, so you must forgive others.

October 24

Biker George says we all need to use self-control with the remote control. When it comes to entertainment, watch what you watch because what you feed the most grows the most.

Psalm 119:37 (NLT) Turn my eyes from worthless things, & give me life through your word.

October 25

Biker George says, Take time to care for others because God took time to care for us. It could make an eternal difference in someone's life!

Romans 15: 1-2 (MSG) Those of us who are strong & able in the faith need to step in & lend a hand to those who falter, & not just do what is most convenient for us. Strength is for service, not status. Each one of us needs to look after the good of the people around us, asking ourselves, "How can I help?"

October 26

Biker George knows that it wasn't the nails that actually held Jesus on the cross. It was the love He had for us.

Romans 5:8 (KJV) But God commendeth his love toward us, in that, while we were yet sinners, Christ died for us.

Matthew 16:26 (NLT) & what do you benefit if you gain the whole world but lose your own soul?

October 27

Biker George has found that worrying can have harmful effects on your health, like making you tired, stressed, age faster, & more. Worrying never helps a situation get better. When you can trust that God has a perfect plan & give Him your worries, you can stop worrying. He's got this!

1 Peter 5:7 (NLT) Give all your worries & cares to God, for he cares about you.

Philippians 4:6-7 (NLT) Don't worry about anything; instead, pray about everything. Tell God what you need, & thank him for all he has done. Then you will experience God's peace, which exceeds anything we can understand. His peace will guard your hearts & minds as you live in Christ Jesus.

October 28

Biker George knows that Jesus tells us in the Word that God knows our needs, & if we seek His kingdom first His provisions will be ours. We can trust Him because He meant what He said!

Luke 12:31 (NLT) Seek the Kingdom of God above all else, & he will give you everything you need.

Matthew 5:16 (KJV) Let your light so shine before men, that they may see your good works, & glorify your Father which is in heaven.

October 29

Biker George says, If God seems far away from you, even though you are trusting in Him & trying to do His will, don't despair. Talk to Him about it. Keep doing what you know is right. The light will break through. And when it does, you'll be greatly better for it. If you're in a tunnel of discouragement, keep riding toward the light.

John 14:27 (NLT) I am leaving you with a gift - peace of mind & heart. And the peace I give is a gift the world cannot give. So don't be troubled or afraid.

October 30

Biker George would rather scare you to heaven than to soothe you to hell.

Revelation 20:15 (KJV) And whosoever was not found written in the book of life was cast into the lake of fire.

October 31

Biker George heard it once said that we should deal with other's faults as gently as if they were our own.

Galatians 6:1-3 (NLT) Dear brothers & sisters, if another believer is overcome by some sin, you who are godly should gently & humbly help that person back onto the right path. And be careful not to fall into the same temptation yourself. Share each other's burdens, & in this way obey the law of Christ. If you think you are too important to help someone, you are only fooling yourself. You are not that important

November 1

Biker George tries his best at managing negotiations, handling people & situations with tact so that there is little or no ill will. But sometimes diplomacy may be saying "good doggie" while looking for a bigger stick. The big stick (BIBLE) is very useful in showing us truth, exposing our rebellion, correcting our mistakes, training us to live God's way, & more in love.

2 Timothy 3:16 (KJV) All scripture is given by inspiration of God, & is profitable for doctrine, for reproof, for correction, for instruction in righteousness.

Psalm 119:37 (NLT) Turn my eyes from worthless things, & give me life through your word.

November 2

Biker George has learned that the true art of conversation is not just saying the right thing at the right time, but also not saying the wrong thing at the wrong time.

Proverbs 12:18 (GW) Careless words stab like a sword, but the words of wise people bring healing.

November 3

Thanking God for & praying for those who served, serving, & will be deployed. Tell a Veteran thanks today....

Joshua 1:9 (NLT) This is my command – be strong & courageous! Do not be afraid or discouraged. For the LORD your God is with you wherever you go.

November 4

A marching band that keeps in step with the leader in perfect harmony is an awesome thing to watch. It's sortta like group rides where we all are riding in a pack as one body. Biker George says that when we follow in the Lord's footsteps that He turns our ordinary lives into extraordinary!

Psalm 26:2-3 (MSG) Examine me, God, from head to foot, order your battery of tests. Make sure I'm fit inside & out So I never lose sight of your love, But keep in step with you, never missing a beat.

November 5

After Humpty Dumpty had his great fall, He was gonna give up on it all. Then to the rescue came our Lord Savior, & finally Humpty had found him some favor. Biker George says that in real life the only one who can put broken lives back together is our Lord God.

Colossians 1:20 (MSG) ...all the broken & dislocated pieces of the universe - people & things, animals & atoms - get properly fixed & fit together in vibrant harmonies, all because of his death, his blood that poured down from the Cross.

November 6

Biker George noted that today is Zig Ziglar's birthday who was quoted as saying "If God would have wanted us to live in a permissive society He would have given us Ten Suggestions & not Ten Commandments."

Galatians 2:20 (NLT) My old self has been crucified with Christ. It is no longer I who live, but Christ lives in me. So I live in this earthly body by trusting in the Son of God, who loved me & gave himself for me.

November 7
Biker George knows that Jesus tells us in the Word that God knows our needs, & if we seek His kingdom first His provisions will be ours. We can trust Him because He meant what He said!
Luke 12:31 (NLT) Seek the Kingdom of God above all else, & he will give you everything you need.

November 8
Biker George heard it said that even if you are on the right track, you'll get run over if you just sit there!
Mark 16:15 (KJV) & he said unto them, Go ye into all the world, & preach the gospel to every creature!

November 9
Biker George remembers many years ago when he was a kid at the fair & saw cotton candy for the 1st time! He was so hungry & it looked so good! He liked the taste, but it didn't satisfy his hunger because it was cotton candy! In real life, don't settle for spiritual cotton candy when only Jesus Christ can satisfy our spiritual hunger.
John 6:35 (KJV) & Jesus said unto them, I am the bread of life: he that cometh to me shall never hunger; & he that believeth on me shall never thirst.

November 10
Biker George use to be a gambling man back in the day. Some people say if you don't play, you can't win. Remember if you don't play, you can't lose. Don't gamble on your eternity. God always performs what He promises!
Romans 10:13 (NLT) For "Everyone who calls on the name of the Lord will be saved."

November 11
Biker George started working out in the gym to build his muscles. This could be compared to our faith is built when we exercise it during trials.
James 1:3 (KJV) Knowing this, that the trying of your faith worketh patience.

November 12

What would happen if people spent as much time with the Lord seeking His Face & reading His Book instead of all the time they spend on social media sites like Facebook? Biker George says it's time to get our priorities in line.

Psalm 27:8 (GW) When you said, "Seek my face," my heart said to you, "O Lord, I will seek your face."

November 13

When it comes to Elections & voting, a very long time ago there was a vote that changed everything forever.

Matthew 27:21-22 (AMP) The governor said to them, "Which of the two do you wish me to set free for you?" & they said, "Barabbas." Pilate said to them, "Then what shall I do with Jesus who is called Christ?" They all replied, "Let Him be crucified!"

November 14

Biker George wants faith as strong as the spider's web! He just found out that according to Wikipedia the tensile strength of spider silk is greater than the same weight of steel & has much greater elasticity. Its microstructure is under investigation for potential applications in industry, including bullet-proof vests & artificial tendons.

1 John 5:5 (NLT) & who can win this battle against the world? Only those who believe that Jesus is the Son of God.

November 15

When you receive Jesus Christ as Lord & Savior, you also are a stockholder in the treasures of heaven.

Matthew 6:21(NLT) Wherever your treasure is, there the desires of your heart will also be.

November 16

To make something of your life, give your life to God.

Psalm 32:8 (NLT) The LORD says, "I will guide you along the best pathway for your life. I will advise you & watch over you."

November 17

Biker George wondered what if we treated our Bible like we treat our cellphone?

...we carried it with us all the time.

...we flipped through it several times a day.

...when we forgot it – we'd go back & get it.

...we used it to receive messages from the text.

...we treated it like we couldn't live without it.

...we gave it to our children as a gift.

...we never traveled without it.

...we always referred our friends & acquaintances to it.

...we used it in case of emergency.

By the way... Jesus is calling... You gonna answer?

Revelation 3:20 (NLT) "Look! I stand at the door & knock. If you hear my voice & open the door, I will come in, & we will share a meal together as friends.

November 18

If you run to the altar on Sunday then back to sin on Monday, do you think you can tell heaven from hell? Biker George says if you got saved just for fire insurance, you're missing out on a lot of benefits that the Lord gave you! Give up the dog food. The battle is over, Christ has won!

Proverbs 26:11 (KJV) As a dog returneth to his vomit, so a fool returneth to his folly.

1 Corinthians 15:57 (KJV) But thanks be to God, which giveth us the victory through our Lord Jesus Christ.

November 19

To show the warmth of Christ's love, let Him light a fire within your soul!

Psalm 51:10 (KJV) Create in me a clean heart, O God; & renew a right spirit within me.

November 20

Biker George was thinking about a Bible story where Jesus went to Jericho & there was this little guy named Zacchaeus who was a tax collector. Zach climbed a tree so he could see Jesus. Jesus never met Zacchaeus before, but called him by name. He wanted to hang out & eat with him at his house. After Jesus called his name, Zach was a changed man!

The Lord knows you... Do you know Him?

Isaiah 43:1 (NLT) ...I have called you by name; you are mine.

November 21

Life has many choices. Eternity has two. What's yours?

Deuteronomy 30:19 (NLT) Today I have given you the choice between life & death, between blessings & curses. Now I call on heaven & earth to witness the choice you make. Oh, that you would choose life, so that you & your descendants might live!

November 22

Biker George says that when you feel hopeless, look to the God of hope!

Romans 15:13 (KJV) Now the God of hope fill you with all joy & peace in believing, that ye may abound in hope, through the power of the Holy Ghost.

November 23

Biker George is going to write a book someday & thought about the books that men make are nothing compared to the book that makes men.

Matthew 19:26 (GW) Jesus looked at them & said, "It is impossible for people to save themselves, but everything is possible for God."

Hebrews 4:12 (KJV) For the word of God is quick, & powerful, & sharper than any two edged sword, piercing even to the dividing asunder of soul & spirit, & of the joints & marrow, & is a discerner of the thoughts & intents of the heart.

November 24

Biker George says that the Bible can be compared to the ocean. You can swim & wade in it, feed from it, live on it, or drown in it. But ya know those that take the time to learn its truths & practice them will be changed forever.

Isaiah 40:8 (KJV) The grass withereth, the flower fadeth: but the word of our God shall stand for ever.

James 1:3 (KJV) Knowing this, that the trying of your faith worketh patience.

November 25

Back in the day Biker George remembers a missionary raising funds to go overseas. One of the missionary's friends told him that he doesn't have the money to support overseas mission work & that he only supports mission work here. When the missionary went back to see his friend he found that his house was just decorated with around $1,000 of new holiday decorations.

Luke 12:34 (KJV) For where your treasure is, there will your heart be also.

John 12:4-6 (NLT) But Judas Iscariot, the disciple who would soon betray him, said, "That perfume was worth a year's wages. It should have been sold & the money given to the poor." Not that he cared for the poor - he was a thief, & since he was in charge of the disciples' money, he often stole some for himself.

November 26

Biker George was riding down the road & noticed his gas tank was on EMPTY so he pulled over & filled it up with high octane. He had choices to make at the gas station... Diesel, regular, mid-grade, or premium. He made a quality decision & chose premium. Diesel would have ruined his bike, just like sin will ruin our lives.

Deuteronomy 30:19 (NLT) "Today I have given you the choice between life & death, between blessings & curses. Now I call on heaven & earth to witness the choice you make. Oh, that you would choose life, so that you & your descendants might live!"

November 27
Biker George rode for miles & was getting dehydrated & thirsty. He thought about how water is to the body like the Word of God should be to the soul!

Psalm 42:1-2 (KJV) As the hart panteth after the water brooks, so panteth my soul after thee, O God. My soul thirsteth for God, for the living God: when shall I come & appear before God?

November 28
Biker George remembers when he was a young buck & lived life on the edge as if he would never die. Living righteously will leave a legacy that will be engraved into the minds of others which in real life is better than the engraving on a tombstone.

Psalm 90:12 (NLT) Teach us to realize the brevity of life, so that we may grow in wisdom.

November 29
Biker George was going to Germany & was wondering what they call their pastors over there? Biker Joe told George that he knew. They call them German Shepherds!

Psalm 23:1 (KJV) The Lord is my shepherd; I shall not want.

November 30
Biker George & Angel sat down together on the couch & started flipping channels. Angel asked, "What's on TV?" George jokingly said, "Dust." That could have started a fight, but they both laughed it off. When we run into messes, the Lord would want us to clean house, not to burn it down. A good marriage requires resolve to be married for good.

Ephesians 5:22 & 25 (KJV) Wives, submit yourselves unto your own husbands, as unto the Lord. Husbands, love your wives, even as Christ also loved the church, & gave himself for it.

December 1

Biker George says, Those who fear God the most fear men the least.

Psalm 115:13 (KJV) He will bless them that fear the Lord, both small & great.

December 2

Biker George says, To avoid being lost for eternity, don't take forever to receive Christ!

John 3:3 (KJV) Jesus answered & said unto him, Verily, verily, I say unto thee, Except a man be born again, he cannot see the kingdom of God.

December 3

Biker George remembers lawyers that would find ways so he wouldn't have to go to prison. Today he realizes that we have the Bible to light our way & the Holy Spirit to keep us strong. If we do mess up, we have Jesus Christ to forgive us.

1 John 1:9 (KJV) If we confess our sins, he is faithful & just to forgive us our sins, & to cleanse us from all unrighteousness

December 4

Biker George says that if we depend entirely on God we find him entirely dependable.

Proverbs 3:5-12 (MSG) Trust God from the bottom of your heart; don't try to figure out everything on your own. Listen for God's voice in everything you do, everywhere you go; he's the one who will keep you on track. Don't assume that you know it all. Run to God! Run from evil! Your body will glow with health, your very bones will vibrate with life! Honor God with everything you own; give him the first & the best. Your barns will burst, your wine vats will brim over. But don't, dear friend, resent God's discipline; don't sulk under his loving correction. It's the child he loves that God corrects; a father's delight is behind all this.

December 5

Biker George remembers when airports had many flights canceled because of bad weather. One old gentleman was interviewed & asked how he felt about his flight being grounded. His answer with a big old jolly smile & chuckle was... "It is what is, so why get upset about it!" Think about it... A bad attitude ain't gonna fix anything. Your attitude affects others, but the bottom line is that it affects you & your health. Smile at someone... It could be contagious!

Proverbs 17:22 (NLT) A cheerful heart is good medicine, but a broken spirit saps a person's strength.

Ephesians 2:10 (KJV) For we are his workmanship, created in Christ Jesus unto good works, which God hath before ordained that we should walk in them.

December 6

Biker George says that in order to make a difference in the world we first have to let the Lord make a difference in us.

Philippians 1:6 (NLT) & I am certain that God, who began the good work within you, will continue his work until it is finally finished on the day when Christ Jesus returns.

December 7

We've all heard the old saying "Those who don't learn from history are bound to repeat it". Well, ya know the Bible has a lot of history of people who made mistakes that we can learn from. We can ask the Lord to protect us from making similar mistakes.

Psalm 119:11 (KJV) Thy word have I hid in mine heart, that I might not sin against thee.

December 8

Biker George says that you can have faith for needs to be met, but how can you put your faith into action today? Faith doesn't stand around with its hands in its pockets.

James 2:26 (KJV) For as the body without the spirit is dead, so faith without works is dead also.

John 3:3 (KJV) Jesus answered & said unto him, Verily, verily, I say unto thee, Except a man be born again, he cannot see the kingdom of God.

December 9

Biker George had 2 house plants that he was supposed to take care of. He watered the one at the front of the shop but forgot about the one in the back. He found out that what you feed grows & what you don't feed dies. This is like our spiritual life. If we seek the Lord we will grow in Him. If He is in the front of minds we will focus on Him. Put the cares & lies of this world in the back room & focus on the Lord instead!

Galatians 2:20 (NLT) My old self has been crucified with Christ. It is no longer I who live, but Christ lives in me. So I live in this earthly body by trusting in the Son of God, who loved me & gave himself for me.

1 John 1:9 (KJV) If we confess our sins, he is faithful & just to forgive us our sins, & to cleanse us from all unrighteousness

December 10

Biker George once said that the challenges we face in life can help build our spiritual health & remind us that we need to depend on the Lord. The challenges we face should make us better not bitter.

James 1:2-4 (MSG) Consider it a sheer gift, friends, when tests & challenges come at you from all sides. You know that under pressure, your faith-life is forced into the open & shows its true colors. So don't try to get out of anything prematurely. Let it do its work so you become mature & well-developed, not deficient in any way.

Proverbs 3:5-12 (MSG) Trust God from the bottom of your heart;

December 11

Biker George has a friend that was blind for years because he had cataracts at a young age. A few weeks ago, a doctor removed the cataract from one of his eyes & he could see! The sad thing is that he could have had his sight 30 years ago but remained blind for no reason. Don't remain spiritually blind for no reason. When you trust in the Lord, the darkness gives way to light. In John 8:12 (NLT) Jesus said, "I am the light of the world. If you follow me, you won't have to walk in darkness, because you will have the light that leads to life."

2 Corinthians 4:4 (NLT) Satan, who is the god of this world, has blinded the minds of those who don't believe. They are unable to see the glorious light of the Good News. They don't understand this message about the glory of Christ, who is the exact likeness of God.

December 12

Biker George has noticed that a fruitful life is a happy life.

Psalm 92:13-14 (NLT) For they are transplanted to the Lord's own house. They flourish in the courts of our God. Even in old age they will still produce fruit; they will remain vital & green.

December 13

Biker George says, We can come to God as we are, but we shouldn't leave as we were.

Romans 12:2 (NLT) Don't copy the behavior & customs of this world, but let God transform you into a new person by changing the way you think. Then you will learn to know God's will for you, which is good & pleasing & perfect.

December 14

Biker George saw a sign that caught his eye which said "FREE! 3 QUARTS OF OIL WHEN YOU BUY 3 AT THE REGULAR HALF DOZEN PRICE". At first glance it looked like a good deal. But if you stop & think about it, that deceptive ad wasn't really a bargain. You are actually buying 6 for the price of 6 any way you go!

God's plan of salvation is really free. Jesus paid the price. All He asks is that we put our faith in Him. Any other plan is like deceptive advertising. Ya know, if we could earn our salvation, Christ wouldn't have died to provide it.

Romans 4:4-5 (NLT) When people work, their wages are not a gift, but something they have earned. But people are counted as righteous, not because of their work, but because of their faith in God who forgives sinners.

December 15

As Christians we gotta live in this world but not let this world live in us. Living as a Christian should be Christ living His life through us.

Romans 12:2 (NLT) Don't copy the behavior & customs of this world, but let God transform you into a new person by changing the way you think. Then you will learn to know God's will for you, which is good & pleasing & perfect.

James 2:26 (KJV) For as the body without the spirit is dead, so faith without works is dead also.

December 16

Biker George says that sometimes the picture of our lives can be good or bad on the canvas of life. However, we must always strive to be illustrations of God's paint brush, & not of our own artwork.

1 Thessalonians 2:12 (GW) you should live in a way that proves you belong to the God who calls you into his kingdom & glory.

December 17

Biker George says when riding down the road of life, friends can make those rough roads seem like smooth pavement.

Proverbs 27:9 (NLT) The heartfelt counsel of a friend is as sweet as perfume & incense.

December 18

Biker George says that Church tourist season is soon approaching. The Christmas & Easter holidays might be the only time that some make it to church. Ya know, if absence makes the heart grow fonder, some people must really love church.

Hebrews 10:24-25 (NLT) Let us think of ways to motivate one another to acts of love & good works. And let us not neglect our meeting together, as some people do, but encourage one another, especially now that the day of his return is drawing near.

Deuteronomy 31:8 (NLT) Do not be afraid or discouraged, for the LORD will personally go ahead of you. He will be with you; he will neither fail you nor abandon you

December 19

Biker George noticed that he was reaping the consequences of his sins. He did stop the self-destructive cycle & is now making the most of the rest of his life by running back to the open arms of Jesus. Ya know, your present choices decide upcoming rewards. Think about it... The Lord longs to forgive you & lead you in a way of life that reaps His blessing & reward.

Romans 6:23 (MSG) But now that you've found you don't have to listen to sin tell you what to do, & have discovered the delight of listening to God telling you, what a surprise! A whole, healed, put-together life right now, with more & more of life on the way! Work hard for sin your whole life & your pension is death. But God's gift is real life, eternal life, delivered by Jesus, our Master.

Galatians 2:20 (NLT) My old self has been crucified with Christ. It is no longer I who live, but Christ lives in me. So I live in this earthly body by trusting in the Son of God, who loved me & gave himself for me.

December 20   Biker George is a very busy man & sometimes says he can't do it all, but he keeps on trying anyway. He found out that when he doesn't know what to do first, he gives the Lord first place, & everything works out!

Proverbs 16:3 (NLT) Commit your actions to the Lord, & your plans will succeed.

December 21

Biker George says that sometimes it seems as if nobody is paying attention to what you say until you make a mistake.

Proverbs 12:15 (NLT) Fools think their own way is right, but the wise listen to others.

December 22

Biker George remembers many years ago when his school teacher left the classroom. She told the class she was just going down the hall & trusted them to work on their assignments while she was gone. Well... 15 minutes pass, then 30, then 45... Suddenly the teacher finally returned! Many were glad to see the teacher return, but those that were disobeying wish she hadn't come back at all. Ya know, Jesus is coming back! It may be soon. It will be sudden. Is that good news or bad? It's up to you.

Matthew 24:42 (KJV) Watch therefore: for ye know not what hour your Lord doth come.

December 23

Biker George says that even though the world may discount you, in God's eyes you are priceless & that's what counts!

Zechariah 2:8 (AMP) For thus says the Lord of hosts, "After glory He has sent Me against the nations which plunder you - for he who touches you, touches the apple of His eye."

December 24

Biker George has always loved getting free stuff, & the best free gift he has ever received is the FREE Gift of Salvation!

1 Timothy 2:4 (MSG) He wants not only us but everyone saved, you know, everyone to get to know the truth we've learned.

John 3:16 (KJV) For God so loved the world, that he gave his only begotten Son, that whosoever believeth in him should not perish, but have everlasting life.

December 25

Biker George knows that Jesus was God's Perfect Christmas Gift to us & that God never gives anything but the very best!

James 1:17 (KJV) Every good gift & every perfect gift is from above, & cometh down from the Father of lights, with whom is no variableness, neither shadow of turning.

December 26

Biker George doesn't remember what he ate 6 weeks ago & he can't remember what his pastor spoke about 6 weeks ago either. That was a long time ago, but the physical & spiritual food did nourish him! Just like we need food to keep healthy we also need the Bible to keep us spiritually healthy. Ya know, a good sign of being spiritually healthy is a read & studied Bible.

Proverbs 4:20-22 (MSG) Dear friend, listen well to my words; tune your ears to my voice. Keep my message in plain view at all times. Concentrate! Learn it by heart! Those who discover these words live, really live; body & soul, they're bursting with health.

December 27

We set an example for our children & others whether or not we are aware of it. So, we need to be careful where & how we walk! Someone could be following in our footsteps! A child may not inherit his parents' talents, but they usually will absorb their values!

1 Peter 2:21 (NLT) For God called you to do good, even if it means suffering, just as Christ suffered for you. He is your example, & you must follow in his steps.

December 28

Biker George says we shouldn't wait for other people to be caring, loving, bighearted, merciful, grateful, kind, generous, friendly & Godly. We should be the ones to lead the way!

1 John 4:7-8 (KJV) Beloved, let us love one another: for love is of God; & every one that loveth is born of God, & knoweth God. He that loveth not knoweth not God; for God is love.

December 29

Biker George has found that some people are so busy doing good that they neglect to do what's right.

Matthew 11:28-30 (MSG) "Are you tired? Worn out? Burned out on religion? Come to me. Get away with me & you'll recover your life. I'll show you how to take a real rest. Walk with me & work with me - watch how I do it. Learn the unforced rhythms of grace. I won't lay anything heavy or ill-fitting on you. Keep company with me & you'll learn to live freely & lightly."

December 30

Have you ever looked out the window & saw a blanket of fresh snow that makes everything look clean & new? This is what it looks like in the spiritual realm when we confess our sin to the Lord!

Isaiah 1:18 (KJV) Come now, & let us reason together, saith the Lord: though your sins be as scarlet, they shall be as white as snow; though they be red like crimson, they shall be as wool.

Romans 12:10 (NLT) Love each other with genuine affection, & take delight in honoring each other.

December 31

Biker George says that the past is the past & the future is bright when the Lord is your light!

Isaiah 60:20 (NLT) Your sun will never set; your moon will not go down. For the LORD will be your everlasting light. Your days of mourning will come to an end.

EPILOGUE

The starting point for any relationship with God is accepting the free gift of salvation through Jesus Christ. You can't ride with the Lord for eternity if you haven't accepted Him into your life & allowed Him to become your Lord & Savior. Romans 10:9 (NLT) says If you openly declare that Jesus is Lord & believe in your heart that God raised him from the dead, you will be saved. GOD LOVES YOU & WANTS YOU TO EXPERIENCE PEACE & ETERNITY IN HEAVEN THROUGH HIS SON JESUS.

WHAT YOU MUST DO:

1. Admit your need (I am a sinner). 2. Be willing to turn from sin (repent). 3. Believe that Jesus Christ died for you (On the Cross) & rose from the dead. 4. Through prayer (Talking to God) invite Jesus Christ to come in & control your life. (Receive Him as Savior & Lord).

WHAT TO PRAY:

Dear Father, I know that I am a sinner & need forgiveness. I believe that Christ died for my sin. I am willing to turn from sin. I now invite Jesus Christ to come into my heart & life as my personal savior. I am willing, by God's grace, to follow & obey Christ as the Lord of my life.

If you accepted Jesus as your Savior, then this is just the beginning of an awesome adventure with Jesus Christ!

NEXT STEPS:

1. Read your Bible every day to get to know Christ better. 2. Talk to God in prayer every day. 3. Tell others about Christ. 4. Be baptized, worship, fellowship & serve with other Christians in a church where the Bible is preached. 5. Let me know so I can rejoice with you!

ABOUT THE AUTHOR

Dano lives in the south-central part of North Carolina with his beautiful wife T. Family life as a son, husband, father, grandfather, & great grandfather are very important to him. Dano has been an integral part of the motorcycle community for seral years & has travelled worldwide sharing the Gospel of our Lord Jesus Christ. As an author, his hope is that the "Biker George Daily Ride Devotionals" will inspire many to ride with the Lord Jesus Christ every day.

The road of life is an awesome adventure when we ride with Jesus!

Luke 14:23 (KJV) Go out into the highways and hedges, and compel them to come in, that my house may be filled.

The fact that I am a biker doesn't make me a different kinda Christian. But the fact that I am a Christian does make me a different kinda biker.

NOTES

NOTES

Made in the USA
San Bernardino, CA
16 June 2018